TABLE OF CONTENTS

I0505529

THE END   **173**

INTRODUCTION

I started on Instagram **@saverspender** around 2018 because my friend Cat was talking about it all the time and I started getting curious. I didn't have a cellphone, so I couldn't sign up for an account until I had one.

At the end of October 2019, I said to myself: ***Time. To. Level. Up.*** and I set a goal for myself to hit 10,000 followers.

I reached that goal about 6 months later. I learned so many things along the way, via trial and error and this book will teach you all of my Do's and Don'ts.

This book is everything I wish I knew when I first started out in Instagram because I made all the mistakes. I posted 20 times a day, I didn't know anything about hashtags or optimizing anything, and was completely 100% clueless.

Had I had this book? OMG so much time saved.

I wouldn't have bothered with some nonsense I was trying, and I would have had a crash course in how to be a great IG-er from the start instead of taking 5000+ posts to get there (no seriously).

I want you to shortcut all of my mistakes, and be the best version right off the bat, or at least, closer to the best version that you can be rather than experimenting with all the wrong things.

Some of it will sound like common sense, and it is, but it isn't really commonly known until... it's pointed out to you and explained, now is it?

I am going to also assume in this book that you have a business or a blog or something you're trying to achieve with trying to get your Instagram up and going.

I won't be going into too much detail about content or branding as a result. This is an INSTAGRAM-FOCUSED level up book.

Want to see proof?

The minute I started implementing these strategies and experimenting, my IG exploded, just look at that jump at the start when at the end of October 29 2019 I decided I was going to take this IG-thing seriously.

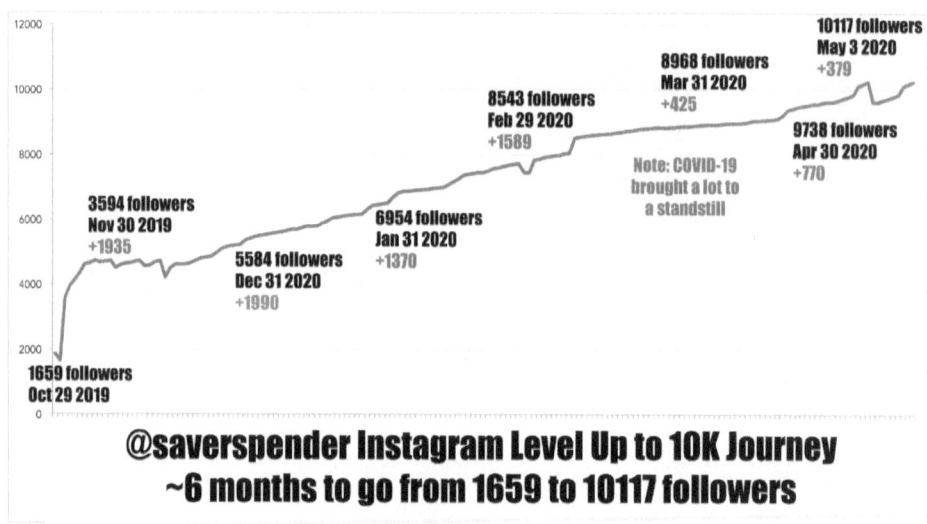

@saverspender Instagram Level Up to 10K Journey
~6 months to go from 1659 to 10117 followers

I went from 1659 followers in October 29 2019 to almost doubling that in one month alone to have 3594 by November 30 2019.

By May 3rd 2020, just 3 days after the end of April, I had over 10,000 followers. Ready? Let's do this.

P.S. — Drop me a line any time, I'd love to hear from you!

Sherry@SaveSpendSplurge.com

Setup

Post

Engage

Tools

Other

SETUP

Set up Facebook Pages

Trust me, you will need it later. Facebook owns IG, and if you plan on using IG, you should use Facebook as your secondary platform.

Set up a Facebook Page for your website/blog/persona and link it to IG.

You can use Facebook Pages to do two major things in IG:

- Set your Business Category
- Manage interactions (comments, replies, etc) on your IG posts that you may miss on your IG history if you're not on it 24/7 checking every 2 minutes

To do this, simply go to Facebook Pages (https://www.facebook.com/pages/create/?ref_type=site_footer) and follow the prompts.

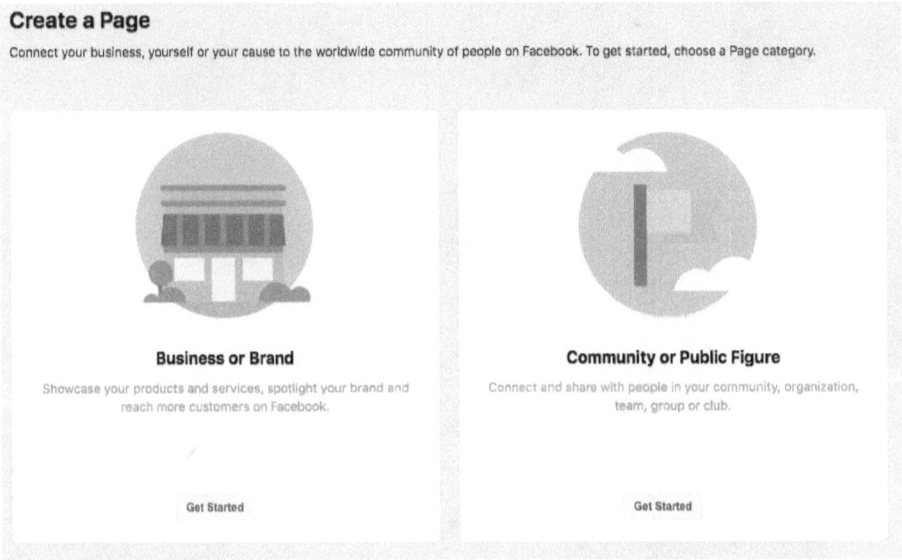

Change your account to Business/Creator

There are 3 accounts in Instagram: Personal, Business & Creator. Basically,

Personal gives you nothing except privacy.

When you go to switch to a Professional account (Creator or Business), it will give you an idea of which one to pick:

Which Best Describes You?

Creator

Best for public figures, content producers, artists and influencers.

Next

Business

Best for retailers, local businesses, brands, organizations and service providers.

Next

Features of Business versus Creator

- Creator lets you choose a different Category from your Facebook Page
- Creator shows you daily unfollows/follows; Business shows weekly
- Business allows integration with third-party social media suites like Tailwind or Later for scheduling; Creator currently does not
- Creator has a "Creator Studio" dashboard

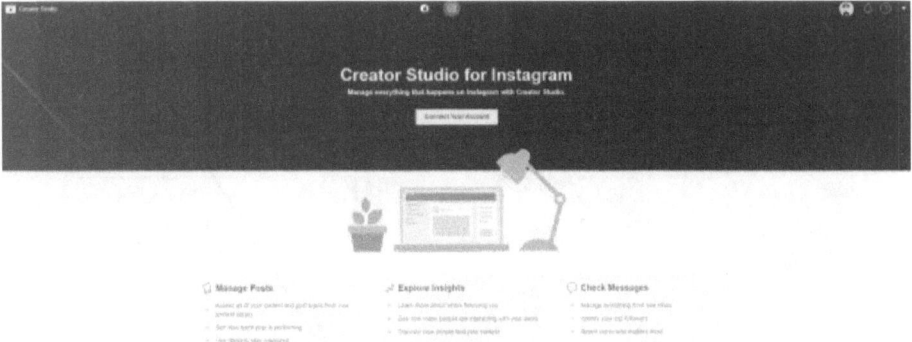

Overall, it looks like Creator is a better version of Business, but the only downside is not being able to integrate with third-party scheduling sites at the moment, which for me is a deal breaker because I need to set-and-forget these posts so I am not rushing to post them in real-time.

How to change your Instagram account

Click in the top right of your Instagram profile to access the **Menu**:

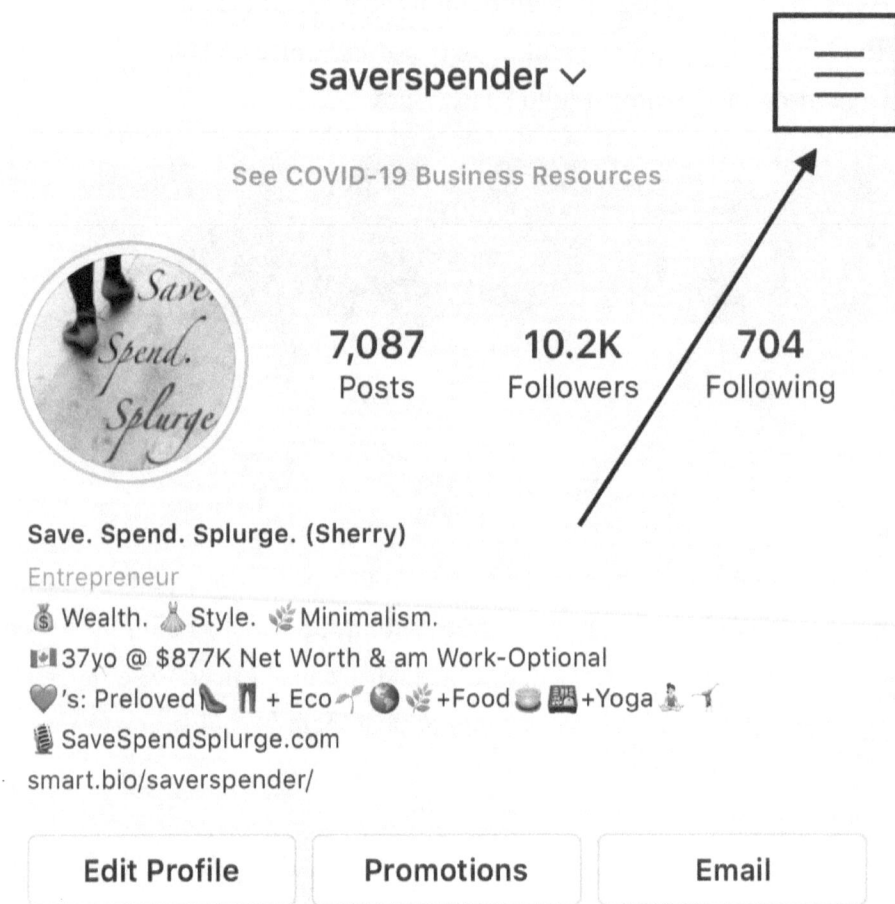

Once you're in the menu, click on **Settings**:

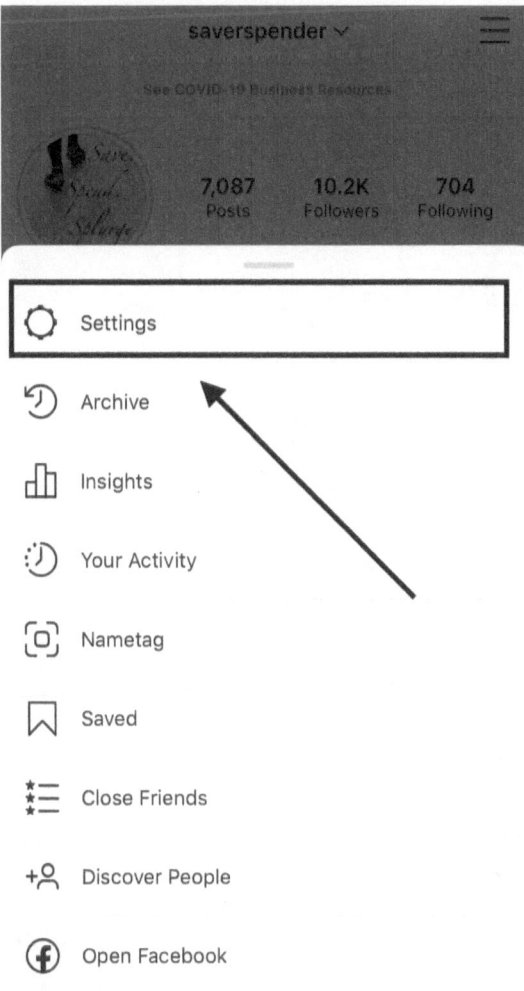

Now click on **Account**:

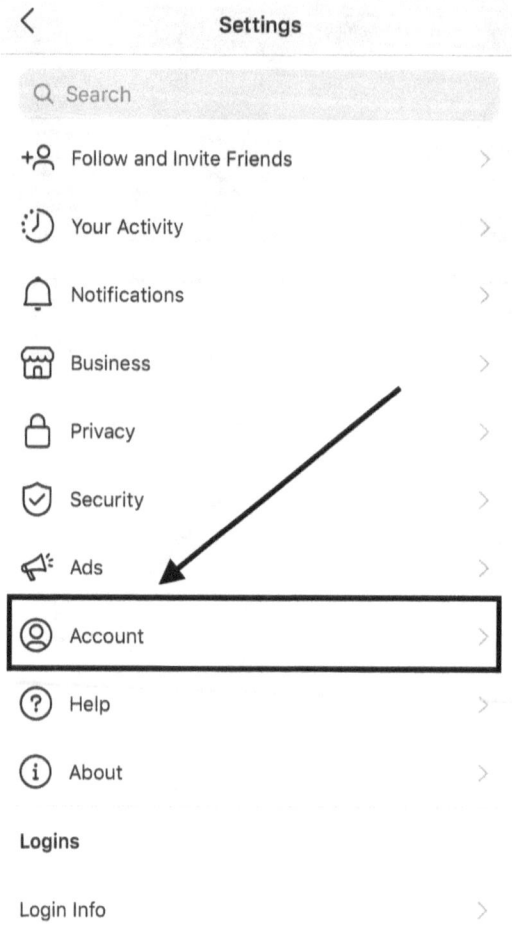

Once you're in Account, at the very bottom you will see **Switch to Professional Account**:

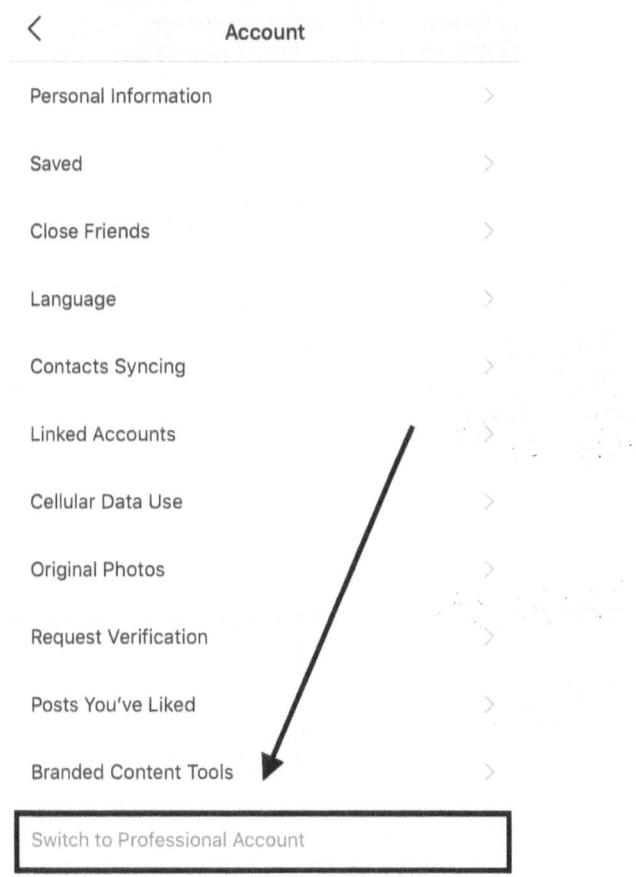

Then the window will pop up to ask you to choose **Creator** or **Business** as shown earlier:

Which Best Describes You?

Creator

Best for public figures, content producers, artists and influencers.

Next

Business

Best for retailers, local businesses, brands, organizations and service providers.

Next

From there, follow the prompts and choose what **Category** you want to be in. For instance, you can see for Business the following:

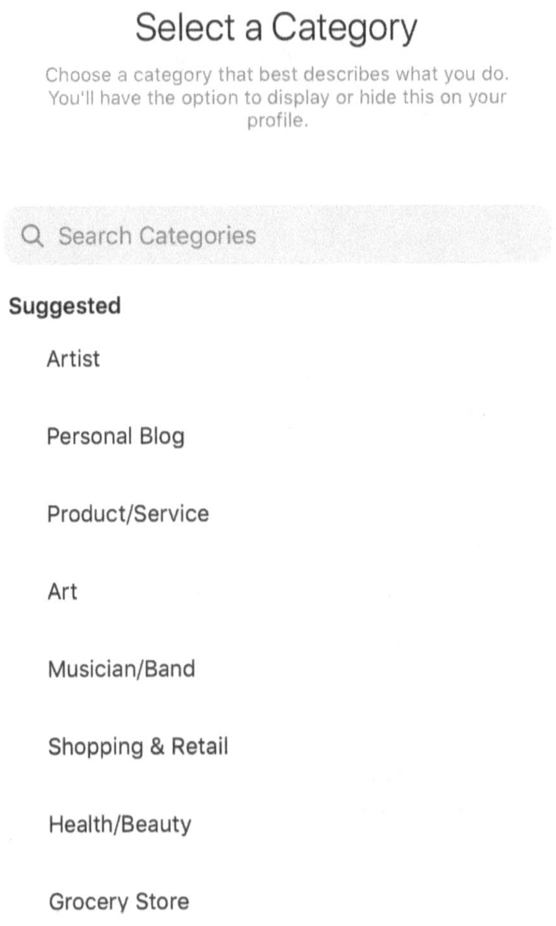

Select a Category

Choose a category that best describes what you do. You'll have the option to display or hide this on your profile.

Q Search Categories

Suggested

Artist

Personal Blog

Product/Service

Art

Musician/Band

Shopping & Retail

Health/Beauty

Grocery Store

You will know you have done it right, if you see the other two options you can switch into. For instance, my IG is **Business**, so I see my two alternatives: **Personal & Creator**

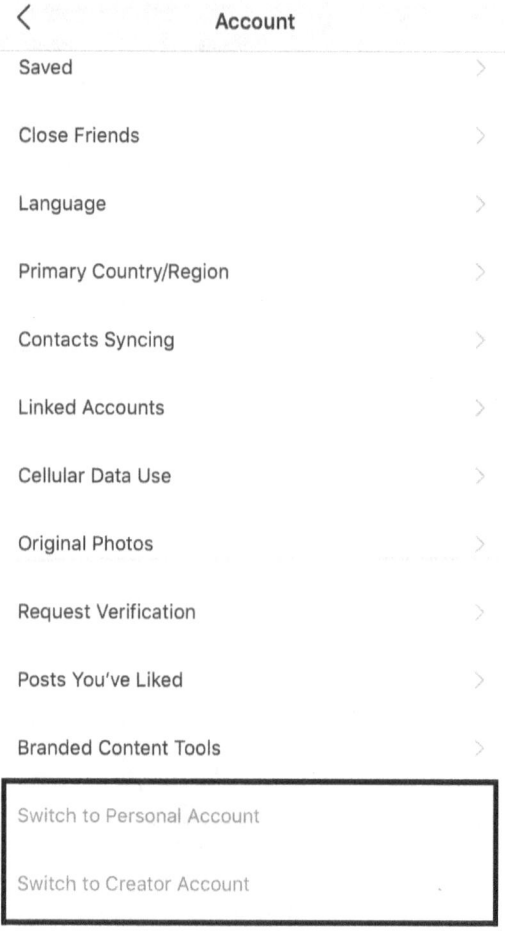

If you ever want to switch back to **Personal**, it will give you this warning:

Switch Back to Personal Account?

If you switch back to a personal account, content and insights from your promotions will be lost. You also won't be able to access insights for current and future posts and stories. You can switch back to a business account anytime.

Switch Back

Cancel

Distinguish your IG profile picture

Your logo should be clearly visible or at least, discernible in a tiny little image on someone's tiny little telephone screen, as Instagram is mainly a mobile-based social media platform.

Instagram is all about connecting on a personal level even for a business - if you want to use your face, this is great if it fits with your brand as it adds a personal touch. I am Anonymous so the header for my blog looks like this:

So I created an avatar that merged the two together in a cohesive manner:

I split the words out to take up as much real estate in the image as possible along with those signature red heels, and I got rid of the byline to keep it clean.

What you want to avoid is a generic image, unrecognizable, and/or too similar to everyone else's, and that includes just typing a name. If you take a look at some IG handles, look and see what jumps out:

Remember that you are a tiny little circle in a list of other accounts, and the urge for someone to click on **Follow** on a whim or not, has a lot to do with what they see as your image.

Just the way you shop for books by looking at their cover, you choose to follow someone or not (sometimes) just by the profile photo.

The most memorable ones will be simple, and not too busy yet also unique. Any profiles with your face should be against a clear or an interesting background with your face taking up 1/3 more of the profile circle so it is at least recognizable at a glance when someone scrolls by your profile.

Let's look at these IG profiles showing their face:

Please note: I am only judging their IG picture profile NOT THEM as people. They are very likely, lovely, wonderful people.

These 3 profiles are good profile pictures:

You can see their face taking up a good part of the profile picture, and the background is doesn't take away from their face.

The most striking of all for me, visually is the middle one because she dressed for it (her dress is complementary) and her background is interesting without being overpowering. It is also memorable.

The last one on the right isn't a typical photo but that's what makes it cool and interesting.

Instagram is not a LinkedIn platform to look 'professional' and you can have a tiny bit of artistic license with colour, outfits and facial expressions.

These 3 following profiles are nice but they're forgettable:

The one on the left looks like any other generic guy's profile picture.

The middle one looks nice and would have been incredible, but her face is in the shadows so it blends into the background of the trees.

It would have done to have had a ring light or something on her face to highlight her instead of now, where my eyes are going, which is to the background of the flowers in pink and yellow.

The last one, her face is so far from the camera that I am squinting. The colours are bland, the whole look blends in with her hair and face that it looks like one soft muted pastel to me.

It would have been better if she had done more of a torso shot of her shoulders and her face.

Or if she wanted this particular shot, wear something bright, colourful or interesting so that in a glance it stands out immediately.

Now let's look at these IG profiles showing logos:

The first three are distinctive, and striking.

The first one is obviously The New York Times for Fashion, which has a pink background to distinguish it, and the very distinctive "T".

The second one was a logo that wouldn't at first glance be recognizable, so having the words JUICE WEALTHY underneath helped immensely.

The third one is a little blended in white and pink, but it is a clear logo that has its name **bites** front and centre even if I can barely make out the byline unless I squint.

High contrast images and colours work best for a small, tiny profile picture.

Anything that blends in together, or has a muted palette tends to wash away and doesn't catch our eye.

As you can see with the third logo, the white almost blends in with the dusty pink.

These 3 logos are not great for various reasons:

The first one is so pale and generic with all the colours blending in. No font or name to help distinguish it.

In fact, I can't even remember it beside the second one which is equally as forgettable - blissful boards (?) catering which I can barely read because it isn't clear, they would have done better to reposition the logo to say blissful, and then boards underneath rather than trying to cram it all in one line.

The two on the left? They look exactly the same to me in a glance.

The last one is not great because I can't even see read what it is!

Something about Wealth? Wednesday? I have no idea and my attention span on IG is too short to want to figure it out.

If we look at the good & bad profiles and logos together now, you'll see the subtle but important differences come out:

The profile picture in IG is key, it is one of your only chances to stand out.

Craft your bio

Add your subline, your motto, and in a few words, say what you are about.

Make sure your bio is eye-catching enough to make people want to follow you, even just for a while. Mine keeps changing, but today it looks like this:

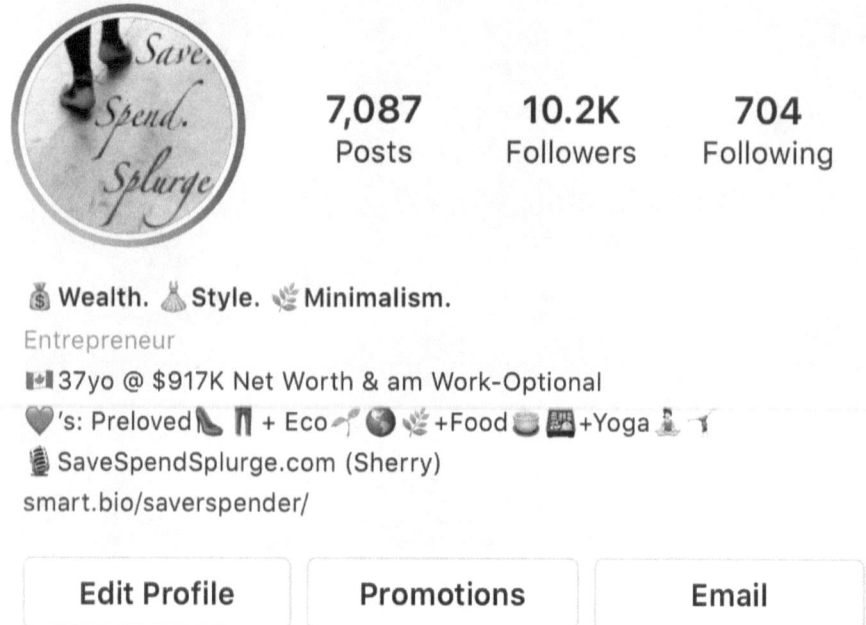

💰 Wealth. 👗 Style. 🌿 Minimalism.
Entrepreneur
🇨🇦 37yo @ $917K Net Worth & am Work-Optional
💜's: Preloved 👠 👖 + Eco 🌱 🌍 🌿 +Food 🍵 📖 +Yoga 🧘 🕉
🔋 SaveSpendSplurge.com (Sherry)
smart.bio/saverspender/

Edit Profile	Promotions	Email

7,087 Posts   **10.2K** Followers   **704** Following

1. Use emoticons
They are fun, cute, and if you use interesting ones, all the better.

2. Change it up
Don't be afraid to add a little personality or whimsy once in a while - some people actually come back to your profile to see updates!

3. Keep it Simple

I struggle with not trying to cram it all in there, but people don't like to read, so keep it as simple and easy to digest as possible.

4. Use your name as a keyword bomb [optional]
If your profile image clearly states your name, consider putting 3 keywords you want to be known for (3 seems to be the magic number for this). I used to have my name as my name like so:

But I recently changed it to my keywords because my name is very clearly in my profile photo already and legible:

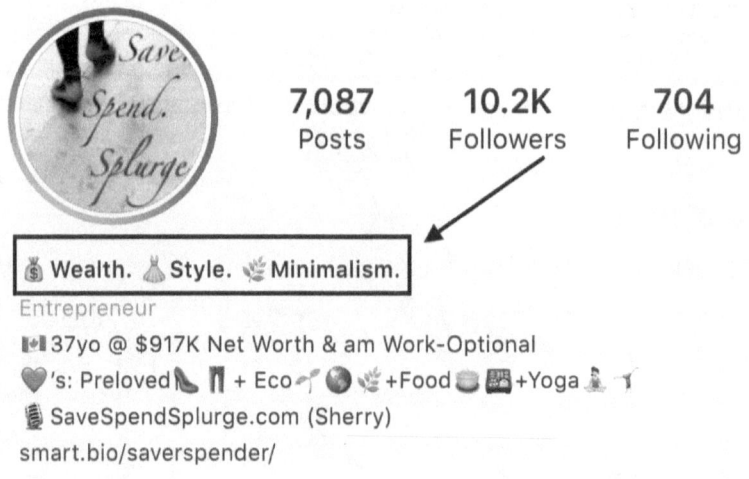

This is a quick "hey this is what I am about in a nutshell" shoutout to new people that is clearly separate from your bio, and have to do it in 30 characters or less including emoticons. I will continually tweak it.

Another incentive to do this, is your name is what shows up as your profile image for Suggested Profiles or even when people do keyword searches on accounts:

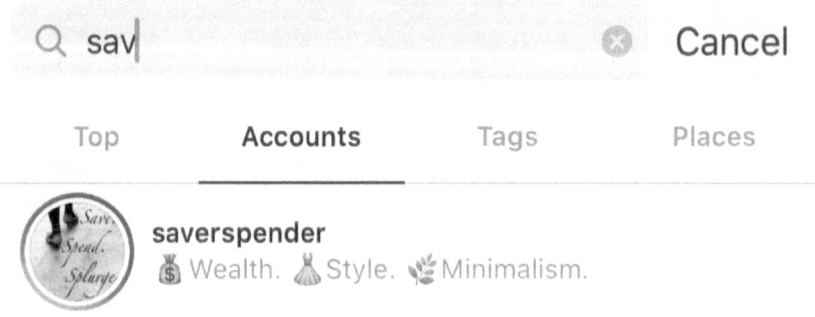

Now instead of seeing your name which they already know
(**saverspender** or **Save. Spend. Splurge.**), they see what your IG is
about in a very short glance.

To change this in your profile, click on **Edit Profile**

And change your name:

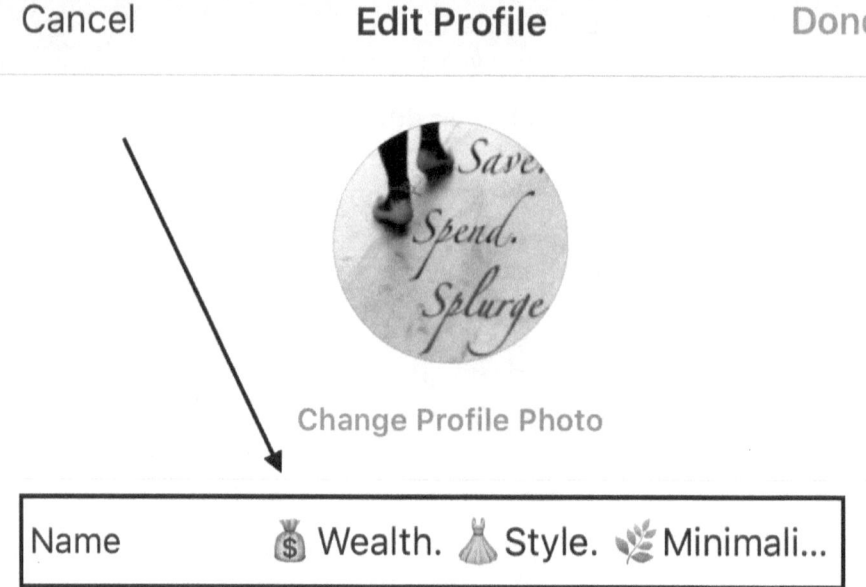

Change Profile Photo

Name   💰 Wealth. 👗 Style. 🌿 Minimali...

5. Always have a bio link / page

Tailwind offers **Smart.Bio**, and there's also **Linktr.ee** that lets you build an Instagram landing page. Both are free.

These bio pages are pre-formatted for cellphone-sizing or viewing also called "mobile-compatible", and not all websites are already pre-formatted to be responsive.

It is also helpful if you do posts and want to send people to specific links or if you have more than one external link to promote that you want people to visit.

My bio link / page shows links to my blog, but also products I sell, popular posts, and other links for easy access especially to specific blog posts:

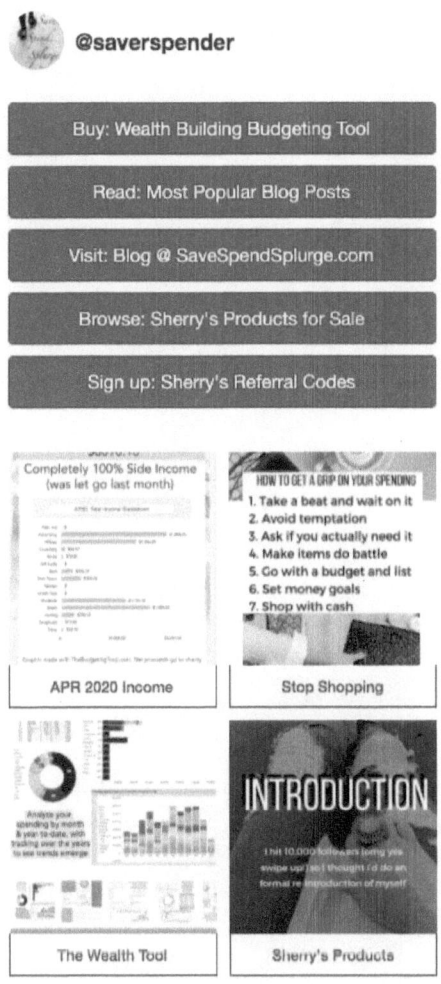

I do this to try and drive some traffic OFF Instagram into my blog where I can actually make some money either via advertising, affiliate sales or selling my books or products.

It does nothing for my revenues that people stay on IG in a loop (which is what IG wants - for people to NEVER leave their platform), as it doesn't translate into sales for me.

Craft your IG grid

The 'grid' refers to the way your posts look in a grid. IG is very visual, so when you go to someone's page you need to turn them into followers by catching their attention, they're going to ask themselves: **Does this look like an account I want to see in my feed?**

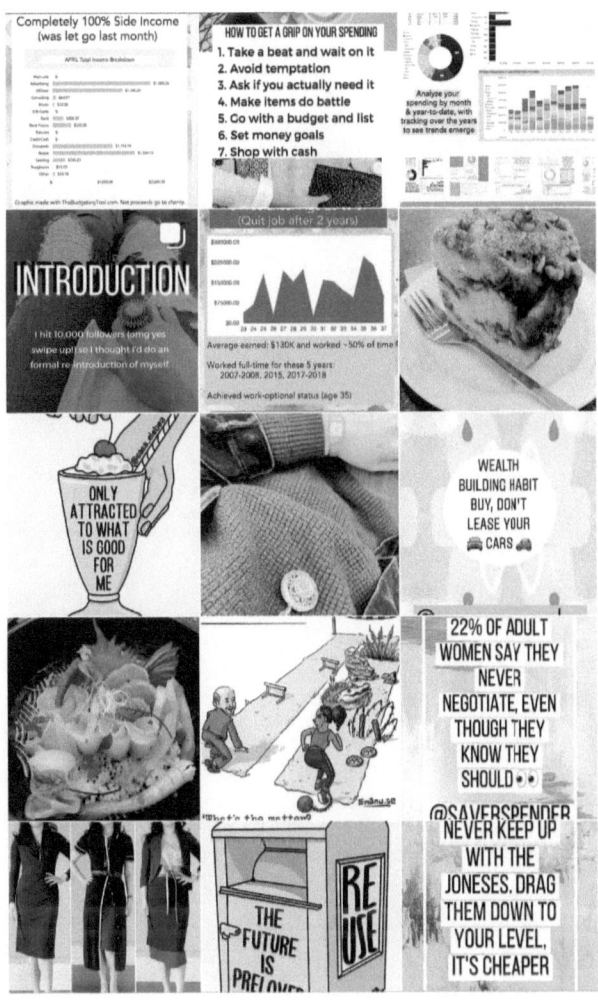

The look I was going for was: **Diverse. Colourful. Informative. Fun.** while still staying true to my 'brand' of what I stated: 💰 Wealth. 👗 Style. 🌿 Minimalism.

There are other aesthetics you can also pick up on, like a monochromatic feel in terms of colour or even a pattern with backgrounds:

Or the same type of images over and over again, like this one on interiors, that doesn't necessarily all look the same but focuses on one core theme:

Or pretty much the exact same image, with variations on it with very few posts deviating from the formula:

IG accounts that don't focus on their grid, can look very dull and unfocused like my earlier attempt to experiment with adding informative posts with food/fashion. It was okay, but it wasn't great.

Personally, looking at this I would have wanted to either follow it just for the fashion or the food, but not anything else. It looks muddled in comparison to the aesthetic I have today with a lot more colour & punch.

It isn't as attractive or as fun as it could be!

These days, I try to come up with a formula for my page that loosely is based on this, posting 3X a day and I am open to changing it based on how I feel people are reacting:

• Fashion or Food
• Quote or Meme
• Informative/Personal

I do deviate from this on occasion and post an extra post, but it is rare and I try not to.

Not one formula will work for everyone, or for even you, all the time. You have to pay attention to what people gravitate towards and analyze why.

At the very least, if your grid is pretty, you will draw them in visually which is half the battle.

Main Message of IG Branding

Imagine that IG people have the attention span of a 2-year old.

They do not want to take the time to 'figure you out', they want to know in a glance if they will like you or not, and this means you have a very short, almost 1-second window to snag them.

Figure out some keywords of what people should feel when they see your Instagram profile picture, biography, image and page, and be ruthless.

There's no point in being everything to everyone because your page will then be nothing to anyone. Even if you get a few disgruntled or mismatched people stumbling onto your page and telling you that you aren't their cup of tea, that is OKAY.

You aren't trying to attract them anyway.

My core target market I keep in mind is women aged 20 - 50 with an income level of at least $60,000 to over 6-figures. I want independent-minded women who make good money or have the future potential to do so, who want to build wealth but also love to spend their money thoughtfully.

I am **not** aiming for the uber-frugal coupon-clipping households either talking about cleaning or penny-pinching because that's not my vibe and we would be a mismatch and I don't want followers who don't vibe with me because they won't read my blog or buy from me.

If I happen to attract outside of my core group, great! If not, fine.

POST

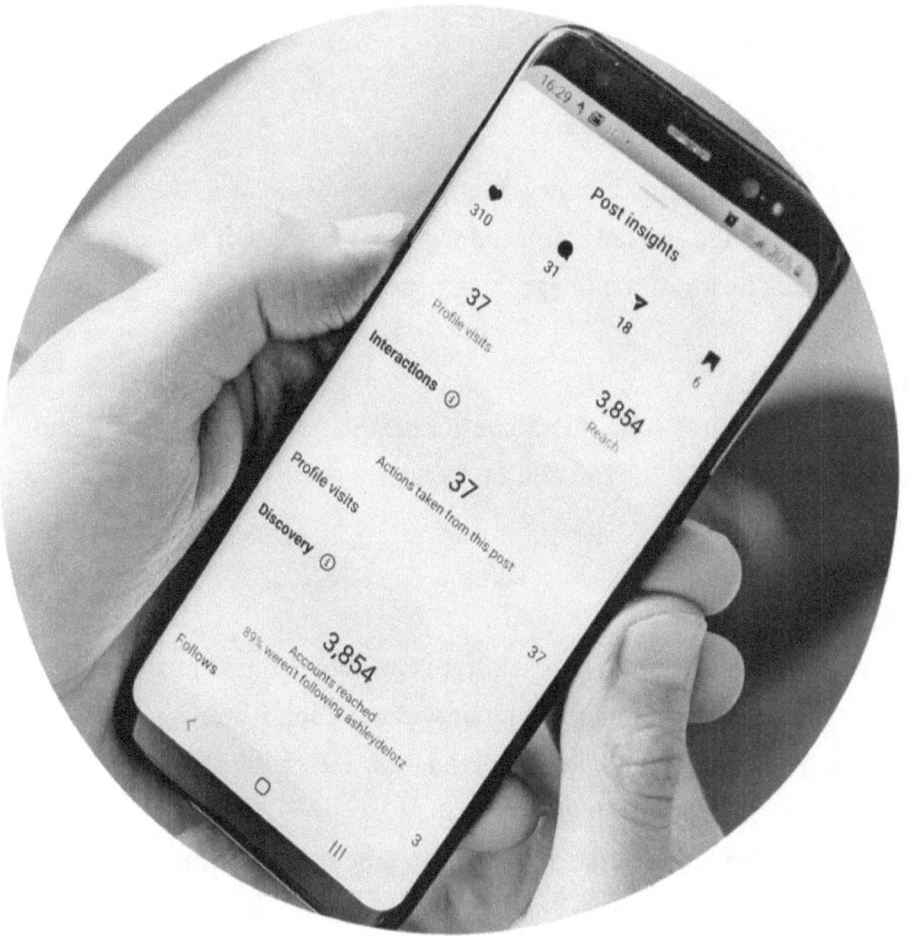

Think about your message

There are three general types of IG posts:
• Short Bites
• Lifestyle
• Informative

SHORT BITES

Known for inspirational quotes, funny memes or sayings, these posts say it all in the image and have no need for a long caption if they don't feel like it. They just post the image, and it speaks for itself.

LIFESTYLE

You post images of style, food, interior design, yourself or your friends/family and/or lifestyle. You don't necessarily need a caption, but you can write one if it makes sense.

INFORMATIVE

You post images that aim to teach someone about something. These require an interesting image, (with or without a lot of words) and a thoughtful caption that people can read, like a microblog.

You don't need to pigeonhole yourself into being **one** of these accounts, you can be a mix (like me), but it is good to know what you are willing to do in terms of work.

The SHORT BITE IG accounts are so easiest to pump out content for because there isn't much to write about but are the most superficial in terms of true engagement attracting likes. The others, take more time but can yield more comments and interest as people write in thoughtful tips, or comments and eventually turn into customers / readers.

Repost oldies but goodies

I wouldn't do this often, maybe once every 3 - 6 months or so, but it is perfectly fine to repost old content that has done well especially if they are evergreen images (e.g. stuff that doesn't get old).

People love graphs, charts, informative pieces of information that help them see things differently, and if your popular posts have done well, change them up a bit, maybe redo them with new colours or a new image, and repost them, or add a variation/new angle to the post itself.

You don't need to constantly reinvent the wheel, and if you see when you repost it that it doesn't do as well, shelve it and try something else.

Always post in Portrait Mode

There are three image sizes or styles of posting on Instagram:

- Square - Most common
- Landscape - Long side rectangle
- Portrait - Long wide rectangle *BEST*

SQUARE

Most common and easiest one to create because… you can't screw up a square, frankly. You can also create Image Carousels with this size.

LANDSCAPE

A horizontal picture that shows more of a wide-angle of something, can also be interesting but it doesn't work unless people scroll on IG sideways and not holding the phone upright in Portrait mode:

PORTRAIT

This is the image size you should always aim for, forever and ever. It takes up the most real estate on someone's phone when they're scrolling, it looks big, beautiful and in your face.

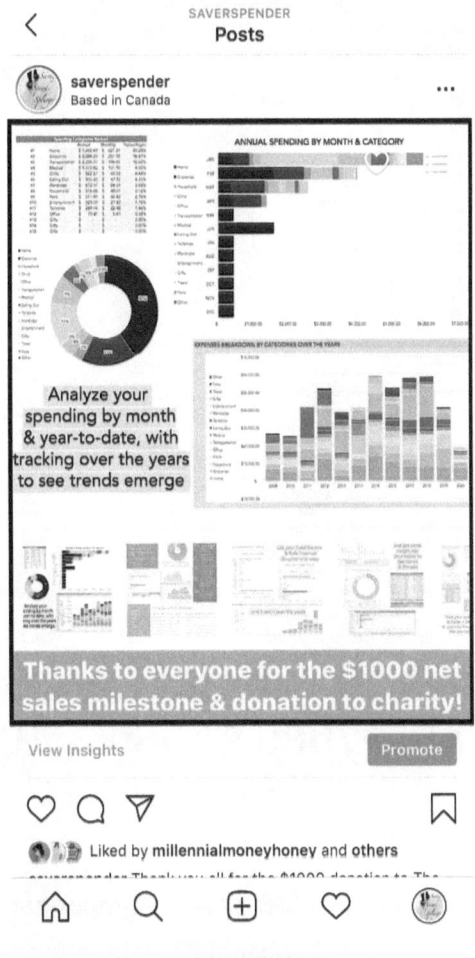

The only downside of Portrait is you cannot create an Image Carousel and must do it in Square mode.

Here is a comparison of the 3 of them side by side of what is seen on a phone when scrolling based on image size.

Just look at the real estate on a phone if you use Portrait!

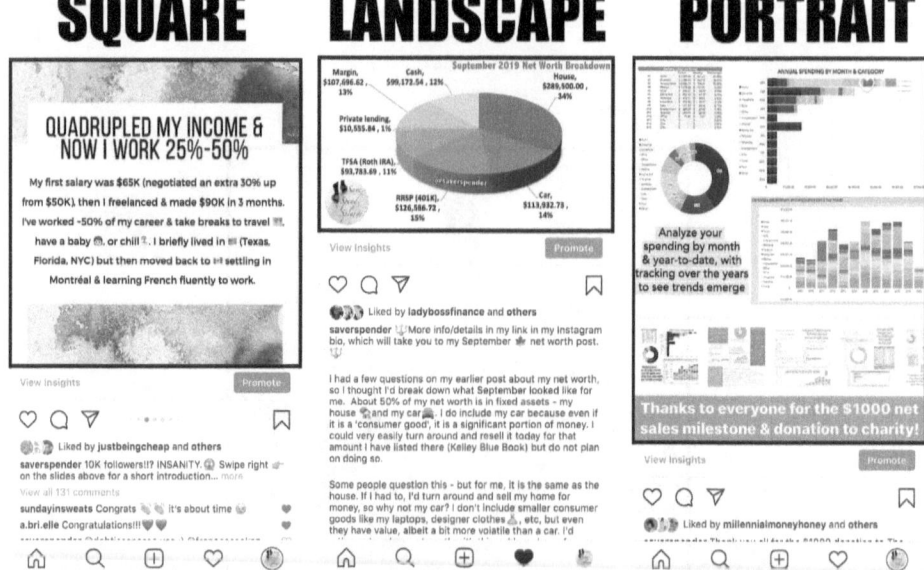

SQUARE	LANDSCAPE	PORTRAIT
1.91:1 ratio	1:1 ratio	4:5 ratio
1080 x 608 pixels	1080 x 1080 pixels	1080 x 1350 pixels

A lot of this can seem very technical but it is important to know. There are tools such as **Image Size** that can help you optimize your image size for the highest resolution and best size possible even if you are taking screenshots on your phone. See: **TOOLS** section 4 of this book.

Create Image Carousels

You don't need to do this for every post, but once in a while, it can be helpful to create Image Carousels. They take a bit more time, but are essentially up to 10 images in one post, which keeps people engaged longer.

I don't use Image Carousels often because I want to drive people off IG to my blog, so I make my blog posts the long informative links to click on.

Recently however, when I hit 10K followers, I created one for an Intro:

To post with Image Carousel, you need to click on the bottom right section to select up to 10 images and it will show you the order in which they are posting:

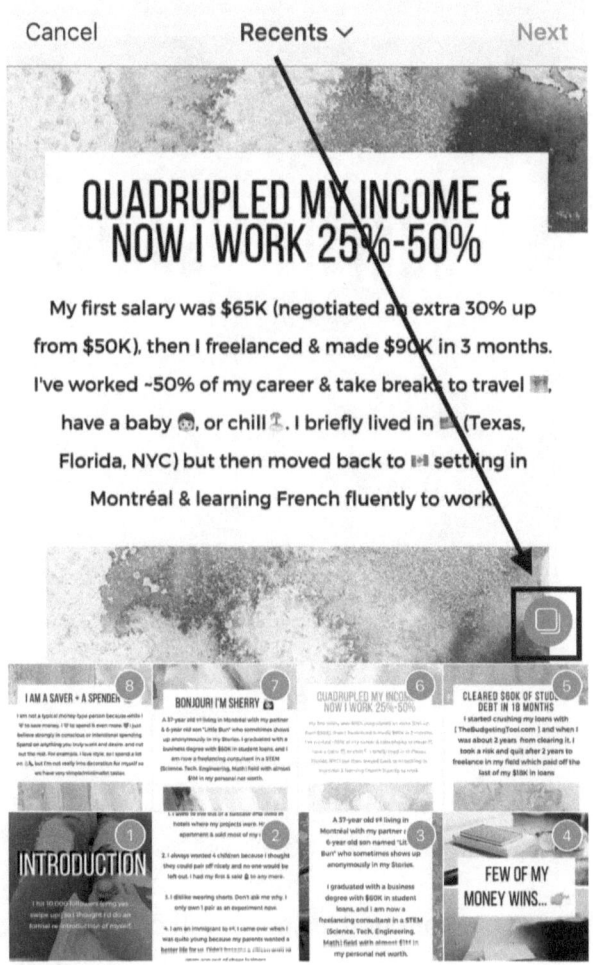

You can tell you're on an Image Carousel post with these 2 indicators:

Either the circles at the bottom that shows you can swipe right for more, or the little tag in the top right-hand corner of the post that shows you how many images are in this post:

My ten slides looked like this:

Remind people to swipe!

You also have to remind people to swipe right, either with the text in the image itself saying: **SWIPE RIGHT!** —>

… or in your caption in the first line:

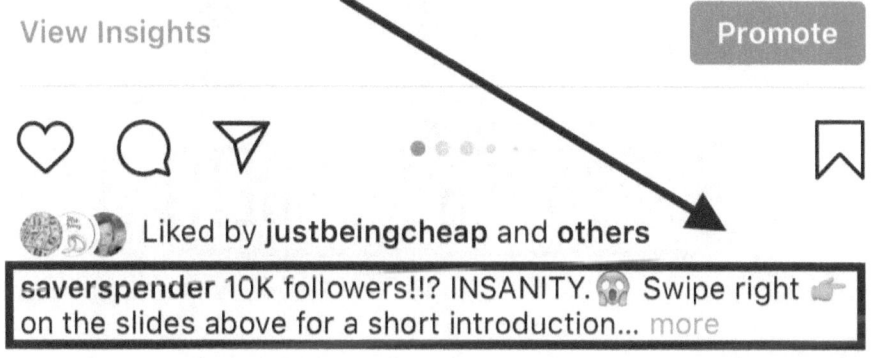

Have your IG tag there

You can just put your tag @saverspender , or write a little blurb like:

Follow me @saverspender for more!

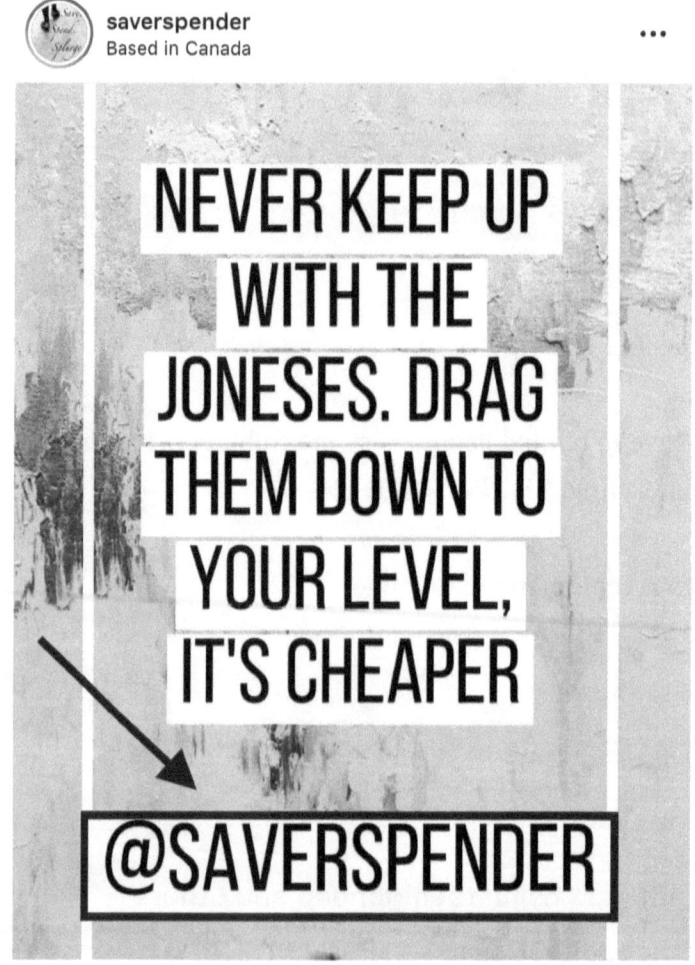

People share posts, and when they share it, they don't always tag you in it, so there is no incentive for these new people to click on the post and come visit your profile.

You don't need to do this all the time, nor will you want to because some posts look cleaner without a tag (e.g. style or food posts), but if it is an informative post that could potentially be shared, tag yourself in big bold letters. I must admit I forget often, so I use templates I created.

Posting Stories

The video/photo aspect ratio is 9:16 and 1080 x 1920 pixels to have a full resolution and fill the entire space completely.

Don't forget about the Instagram name at the top and engagement tools at the bottom of the screen take up some space, so don't put words or tap actions in those locations.

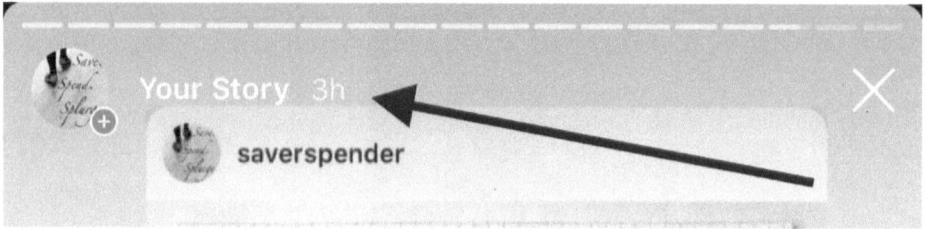

The max video length is 15 seconds. Anything longer will get automatically broken into multiple slides.

If you try to post multiple videos that are each more than 15 seconds long, it will only take the first video, and not the rest.

Tagging people in the image

Another tactic I see that seems to work, is when you post something, you tag similar-minded accounts in the Post or Story itself because it does two things:

1. It sends them a notification that they are tagged in the post

2. The tagged recipients receive follow-up comments of EVERYONE who posts thereafter saying: "@soandso commented on a post you're tagged in"

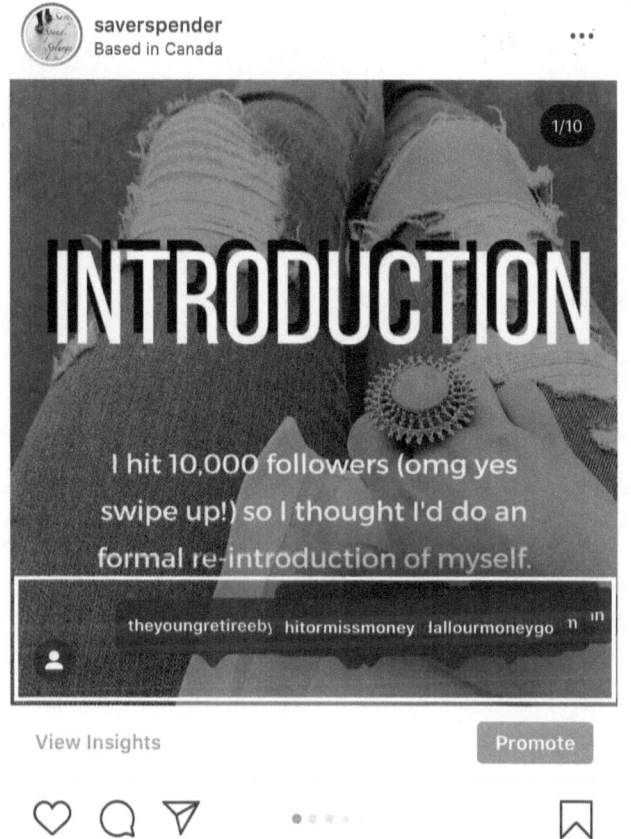

Personally, I don't do this unless there is a point to it, and I am actually featuring the account in my caption, or in my post.

I actually find it a tiny bit annoying when I am tagged in such posts, because it means I am seen as unsupportive if I don't go to it and comment, but then I have to suffer and see all the rest of the comments in my feed.

That said, it can be useful. Like glitter makeup, please use it sparingly.

To do this, when you go to post, tap on:

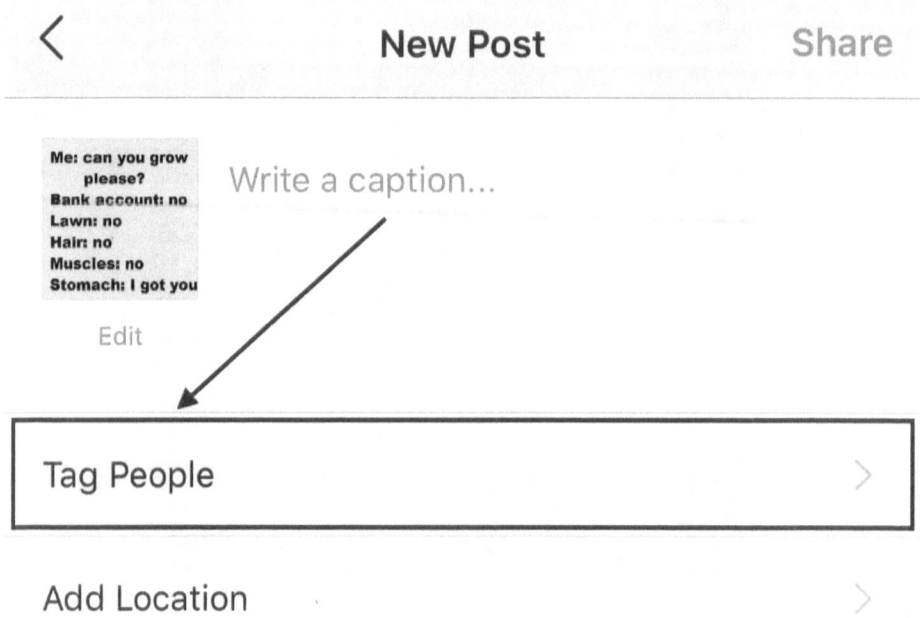

You can also see in your profile all the posts where people tagged you in the PICTURE itself, by clicking on this icon:

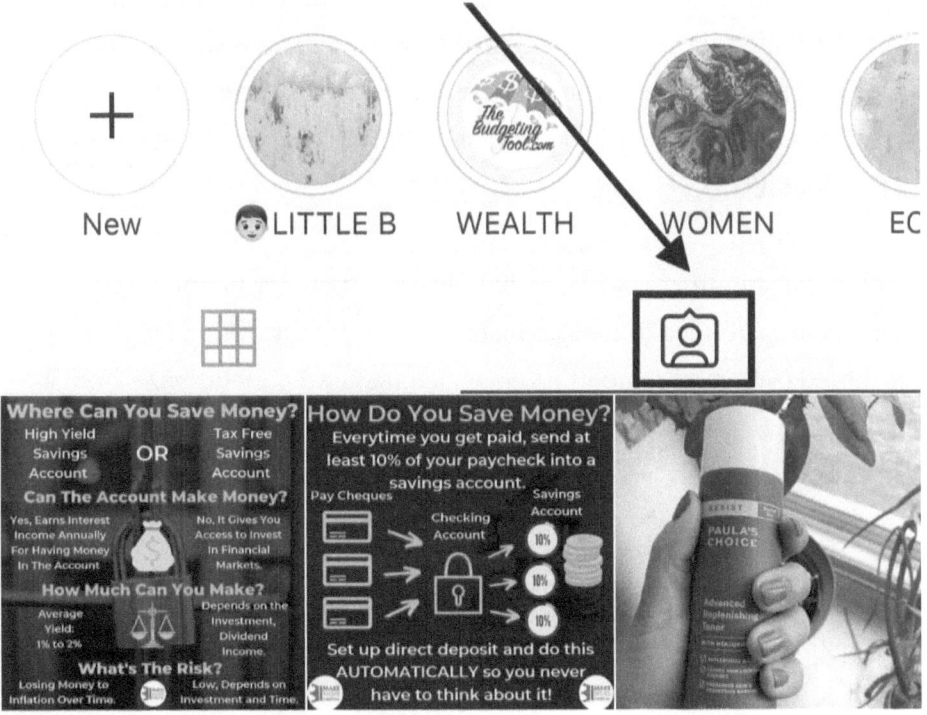

Tagging people in the post caption

This is not the same as tagging people in the post image itself. This just notifies people that you've mentioned them, but there is no way to see a list of past tags (unlike if you tag them in the picture), and it isn't intrusive at all because it gives them a reminder that you tagged them, but that's about it.

If you are trying to engage other brands or influencers to your account, it would be a good idea to tag @bananarepublic if you wore an item, just to get started (you never know! - I was once featured on their page from a tag)

Tagging people in comments

This option is less annoying. If you tag people in comments, that's actually very kind because it means they're mentioning you in someone else's post.

 **thebroke_rph** mentioned you in a comment: That's right! It starts with you trying. The #dfc have been very supportive, encouraging and motivated. Thank you all for your encouragement and support. @saverspender @prescriptions_and_paychecks @wealth.forest @fire_folx @budgetloverrr @dawny.yvette @melannialmoney @debtfreegonnabe @trueventsstudio 2h

So for instance, I was tagged in a caption in this post (not written by the person who tagged me @thebroke_rph), and that's all the notification I get in my feed - that someone mentioned me.

This, I respond a lot more positively towards, and I usually go and respond to thank them. It is less invasive, and a nice way to notify the ones you are tagging without being intrusive.

Hashtag strategy

An Instagram post to a tag with 10M+ posts will get pushed out of the first 9 posts in 3 minutes. You have to be a serious influencer to run in those leagues.

Types	# of posts	Allocation
Popular	1M+ posts	5 hashtags
Midstream	100K posts	15 hashtags
Niche	10K posts	10 hashtags

To start, focus more on hashtags that have 100K posts or less to the tag as a count.

Example: Work outfit
- Popular = #OOTD
- Midstream = #WORKCHIC
- Niche = #MYSTYLEFORWORK

Example: Chocolate Cake
- Popular = #CAKE
- Midstream = #CHOCOLATEFUDGECAKE
- Niche = #CHOCOFUDGECAKE

The more niche and specific you get, the better. You will stand out more in a sea of tags that turnover so quickly, it isn't funny.

Hashtag Ideas

- Product (e.g. #chocolatefudgecake)
- Service (e.g. #coffeeshopcake)
- What are the customers interested in? (e.g. #fancycakewithoutthework)
- Industry (e.g. #cafeswithcoffeeandcake)
- Community (e.g. #bakersofinstagram)
- Events or Seasons (e.g. #nationalcakeday)
- Locations (e.g. #cakemadeinmontreal)
- Daily (e.g. #cakesonsunday)
- Relevance (e.g. #bakerylove)
- Acronyms (e.g. #fotd) - be careful because it could be 'food' or 'face'
- Emojis (e.g. #🍰)
- What do I address or solve? (e.g. #skipthemesseatthecake)

1. Avoid generic hashtags which are usually one-word tags like:
#cake
#bakery
#bake

2. Check out other relevant IG accounts
Steal their hashtags! Or at least see what they're talking about & riff off them.

3. Follow industry hashtags
For your own research, follow *#bakersofinstagram* for instance, and see what appears to get ideas of what to post, etc

4. Be careful with double meanings

#bakedinmontreal may seem to you like "*oh I baked this cake in Montreal*", but "*baked*" is also colloquial slang for smoking weed.

Create your own unique hashtags

I would 100% recommend creating your own unique hashtags early on. You may not be in the big leagues (yet), but you will wish you did this when you want to look back and sort through all of your posts.

For instance, I post about Style and Money, primarily. I should have created my tags ahead of time because it helped me see my top posts, and helped me create my own lists separating out my IG which helped me find specific posts when I needed them. Instead, I thought about it too late, and then had to go back and re-tag all of my old posts as far back as I could.

You can see my **Top Posts** under the tag:

And some other IG-ers have even started using the tag as well as you can see under the **Recent Posts** section where the first left two are not my posts:

Create campaign hashtags

Running a campaign for a week and want to see all of the posts that used that tag as part of your contest? Create your own tag!

Make it super specific and unique, like: *#10daysofbakersgoods* so that when you go to look at the posts, they are easily found and not lost in #giveaway

Use at least 11 hashtags

Without hashtags, it can be difficult to build a following. They help people find you because lots of people follow hashtag threads (myself included), and it puts you in some niche lists where you can see your post be at the Top or Recent.

You need at least 11, as your posts will perform 2.5 times better than just putting 1 hashtag.

Rotate Hashtags in 3 Lists

You can have up to 30 hashtags in a post, but if you keep posting the same 30 hashtags all the time, IG will not show your profile as often because it isn't 'fresh'.

I recommend keeping 3 lists of 30 hashtags each. You can keep some of them common between 3 lists, but really try and make them different.

Another method is to also have let's say 20 - 25 hashtags that are common between the lists, and then add 5 - 10 hashtags that are different for each post.

For example if your post is about a eco-friendly, sustainable bamboo purse, you might want to add specific hashtags to the tags that are more focused to the post itself, such as: *#ecofriendlyfashion #bamboopurses #bamboobag #sustainablepurse #ecofriendlyshopping*

It takes a lot of stress out of choosing tags.

Hashtag placement

This is a personal choice and here are some ideas.

1. Add them in the caption at the bottom after a bunch of "."s

Example:

> *Check out the most beautiful chocolate fudge cake to come out of a cafe in Montreal!*
>
> .
>
> .
>
> .
>
> *#bakersofinstagram #bakedgoodsandcoffee #localcafemontreal …*

2. Add them all in the first comment

A lot of people (myself included) like this style the best because it keeps the caption clear and neat. Just type in all 30 hashtags in the first comment on your post.

3. Add them within your caption itself, and the rest afterwards either with "."s or in the first comment

Example:

> *Check out the most beautiful #chocolatefudgecake to come out of a #cafeinmontreal !*

Whichever method you choose - it is all fine.

Add a Call to Action (CTA)

At the end of every caption, try your best to add what they call a "call-to-action" (CTA) or a reason for people to want to comment on, or vote, no matter what it is.

This helps encourage engagement amongst your followers rather than just posting and leaving it at that - get them to get involved, and turn each post into a discussion between you and a potential base of followers and new clients.

Here are some ideas:

Redirect them to your external link to read more

To read more about my 11 side incomes (YES ELEVEN), click on the link in my bio, this image, and it'll take you to my post on SaveSpendSplurge.com:

https://www.savespendsplurge.com/april-2020-income-budget-roundup/

Note: "Click on the link in my bio and this image" only works if you have a dedicated Instagram page that is linked to something like Tailwind's Smart.Bio so that you can click on the image to read it easily. More link bio options in **Section 4 - Tools**.

For this particular CTA, they would click here and it brings them to the external link to read the post.

Another CTA can just be asking a question, opinion or advice from your followers. Example - I wrote about curbing impulse shopping:

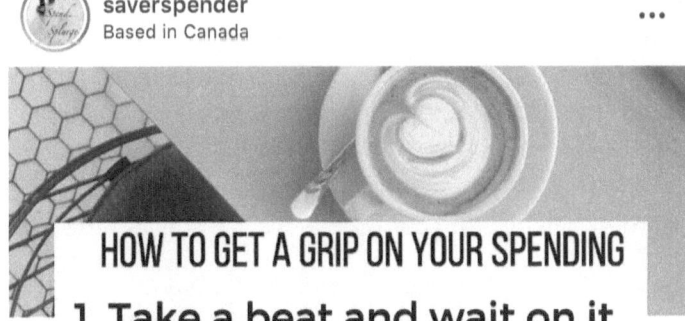

My CTA was simple - asking for advice:

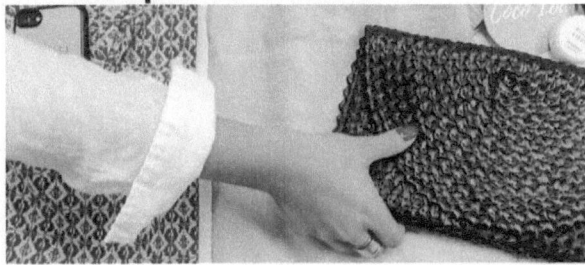

My comment engagement shot up and it was thoughtful:

investingwithkim Make items do battle 😂 I'm just imagining smashing them against each other now

savemycents How often do I wear it? I may love a very impractical dress that would get worn once a year. Love all the tips!

This is important because the comments weren't just single emoticons of:  or any of these other one-off comments, but actual, typed, interesting pieces of advice.

Followers will come to the post now, not see a whole bunch of this in the comments that is quite useless (please don't comment at all in this case). 💪🔥 🔥🔥🔥 💪💪🔥🔥 💪🔥 💪🔥

…but instead, take the time to scroll through the comments, read what other pieces of advice people are giving, take the time to like them, maybe even reply back and engage.

You want your IG page to have people engaging with each other like a mini forum.

You can also have a CTA that is a question for people to answer. I posted this style photo of me in a leather jacket.

I used to post pictures like this and just leave it. Maybe tag a few brands of what I wore.

Or I'd talk about the price of each item, or ramble on about how I don't really wear black, then ask others if they like wearing black. Or not? For the record, Anna Wintour famously doesn't enjoy wearing black either. We are kindred besties, she just doesn't know it yet.....

Now, I craft a caption that is short & interesting of what I still want to say, and put a good CTA at the end to draw people in:

> **saverspender** Toughening up a sweet look is what I love best about leather jackets.
>
> I probably own 7 leather jackets and wear them often.
>
> What I don't love to wear however, are jean jackets. I have tried so hard, and I know people SWEAR BY THEM as staples, but I just find them a bit stiff, uncomfortable, and perhaps.. for my own style aesthetic, too casual, whereas a leather jacket is a little more edgier/chic.
>
> What say you? Leather or Jean jackets?

And again, my comment section is full of INTERESTING comments that aren't single words or emoticons, but of opinions and ideas. Some were quite lengthy too!

> View all 43 comments
>
> **warenjeango** I have both. I like jean jacket when I am wearing a hoodie or a casual dress, like outfit for supermarket. And yes, leather for edgier and chic out with friends kind of vibe. 🖤
>
> **financialfitness__** I prefer the look of leather jackets, but haven't purchased one yet. I have a jean jacket that I think I've only worn once.. I have a hard time styling it 🤭 🖤

In short - CTA every damn post as much as you can, without it feeling forced.

Add external links in the caption

I post a lot of IG posts that have external links leading out to my blog post.

If applicable, you should think about doing the same.

> My income this month was pretty good. I made almost $7000 in side income which is mind-boggling because my consulting day job, almost a decade ago was $5000 a month!
>
> That's crazy that I could make as much as I did a decade ago entry level in my career, in just side incomes alone.
>
> I saw an uptick in advertising and affiliates, and of course, I never spend or cash out the dividends nor the private lending money. It all goes right back into reinvesting, but with a twist this year.
>
> To read more about my 11 side incomes (YES ELEVEN), click on the link in my bio, this image, and it'll take you to my post on SaveSpendSplurge.com:
>
> https://www.savespendsplurge.com/april-2020-income-budget-roundup/

It might sound silly because these external links aren't clickable (again IG operates on a closed loop platform where they don't want anyone to ever leave IG).

I've noticed that adding the external link in the caption is a good idea for 3 reasons:

1. You can easily find what you externally linked to later without having to dig through your IG or blog to find the post again
2. People can go on the desktop browser to your IG & copy & paste the URL easily
3. When you cross-post to other platforms, the links become clickable (e.g. Tumblr, Twitter, Facebook)

Here's an example of my post from IG that went straight to my Tumblr, and the link I posted at the end, is clickable.

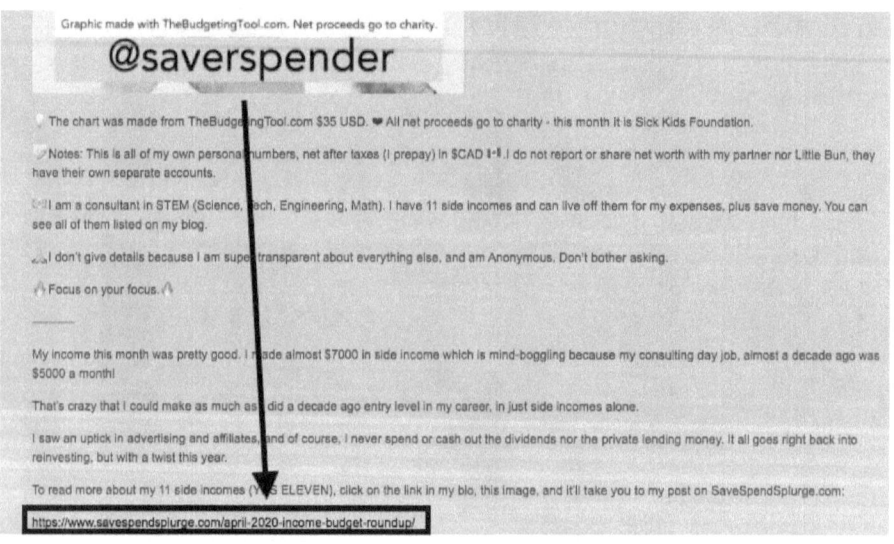

Consider limiting comments to Followers

This is a personal choice but you can limit comments as well to only allow people who follow you, to comment.

The upsides to this:
- Less spammers
- Less nasty comments from those who just want to be mean
- People have to follow you to comment

The downside to this:

If you're a business, do you really want to limit comments to followers?

If it is work to go to your profile, click on it, follow you **and then comment**, it may be too much work for some.

I have personally limited them on my account because the upsides are worth more to me than the downside, but this a choice only you can make.

How to limit comments to Followers

Click in the top right of your Instagram profile to access the **Menu**:

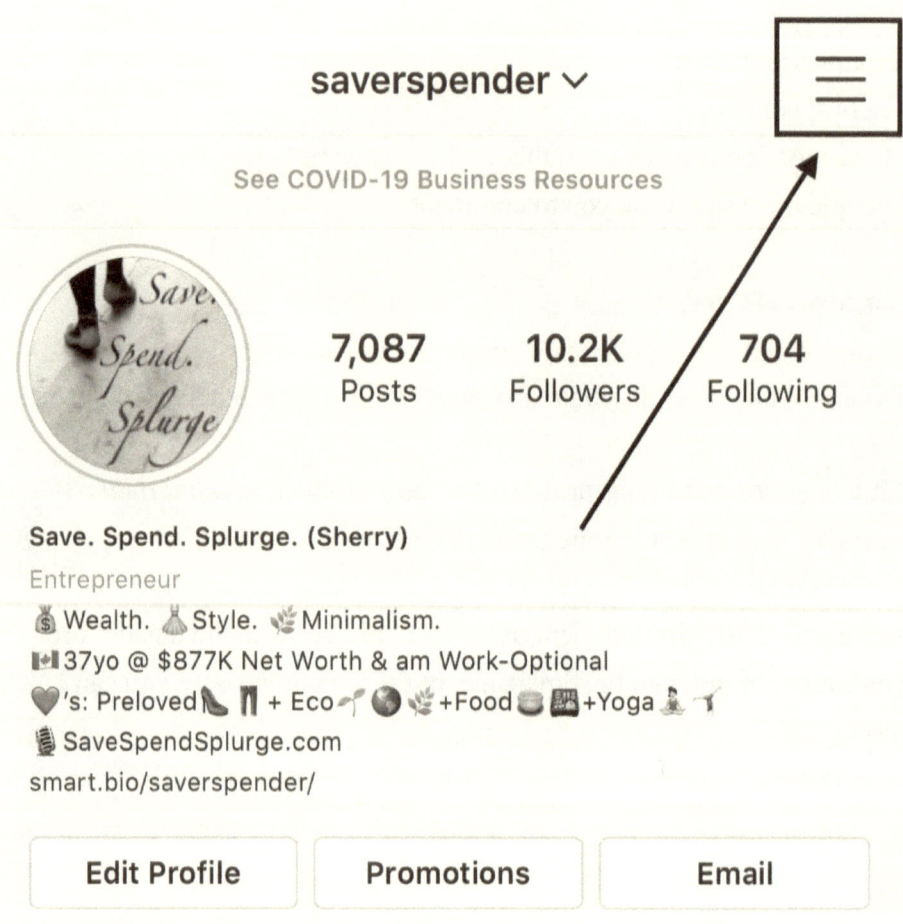

Once you're in the menu, click on **Settings**:

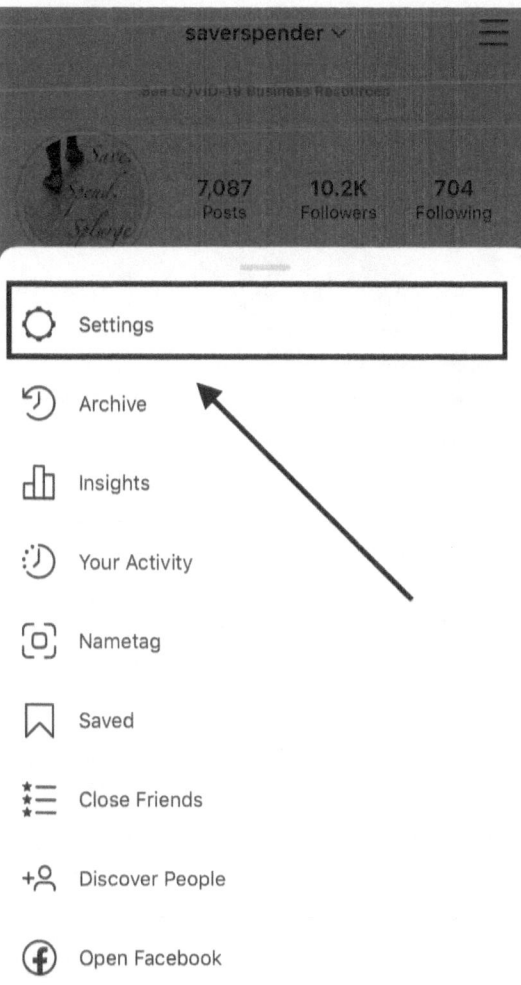

Then click on **Privacy**:

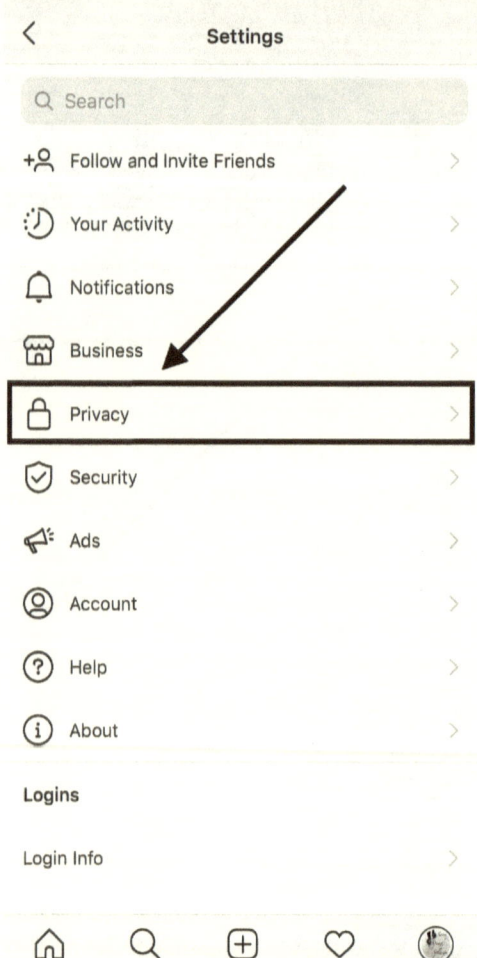

Then in the Privacy Menu, click on **Comments**:

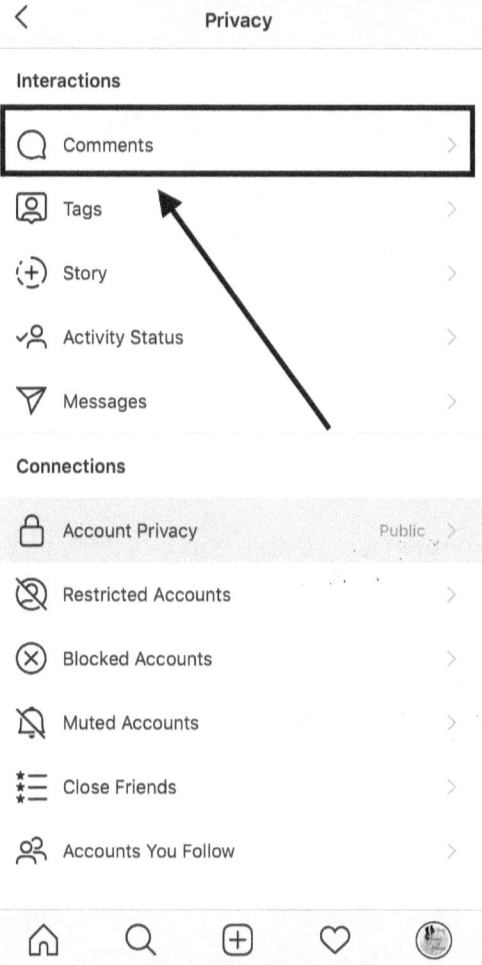

Now in the Comments menu, make sure you select **Allow Comments From**:

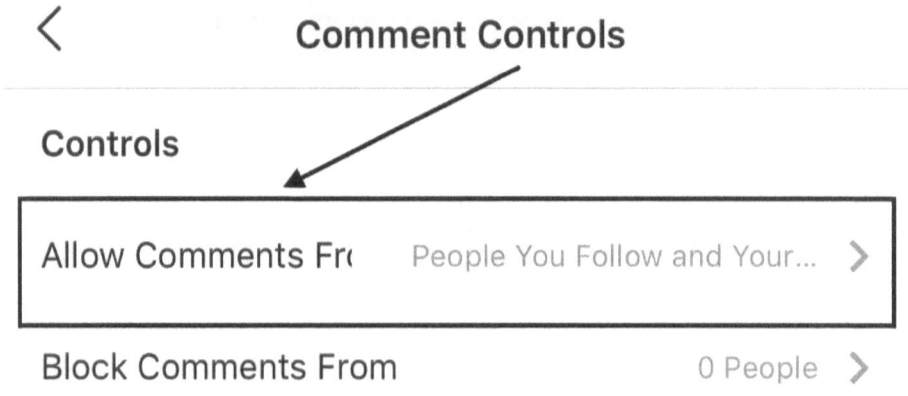

And select from one of the 3 columns.

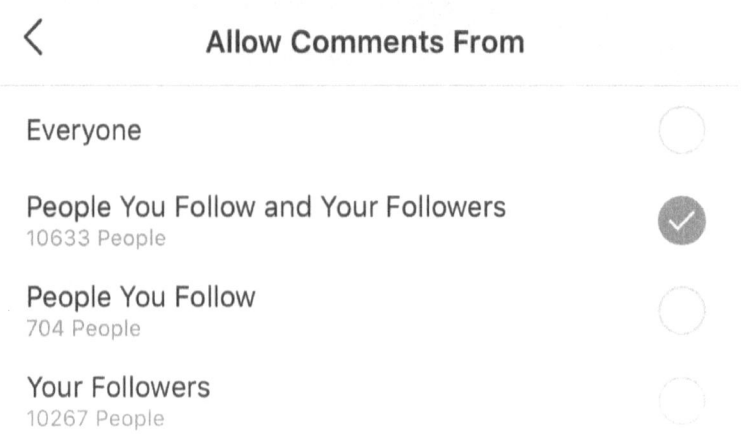

You can choose the biggest number of people, or limit it to just Followers.

ENGAGE

Keep your profile consistent

Stop. Start. Stop. Start.

This is the worst thing you can do to your social media because each time you start back up again, you've lost all that momentum from before that you need to now rebuild back up again.

Especially if you decide to take 'breaks' from social media, and so on - you might as well assume you're back to Square One when you start back up again.

If you are serious about this, you need to stay CONSISTENT and CONTINUALLY ENGAGED, all-in to build this profile.

You have to decide if you want to post once a day or 3 times a day. IG isn't like blogging, where you can post once a week and people know your website so they'll come when a new post is out.

IG is a jungle madhouse of posts all competing for everyone's attention all at once, and if you don't post at least once a day on your profile and once a day on your Stories, you won't see any traction.

You have to commit to this. I cannot emphasize consistency enough.

Respond to every comment

Take the time to respond to every comment. There are some comments that are single emoticons or words, but always try to at least like them. If there is someone who makes a real effort and writes a detailed or thoughtful comment, longer than a word or an emoticon, take this opportunity to draw them out. Engage them and ask them a question, or comment on something that will make them respond back to you.

For instance, I posted this about negotiation:

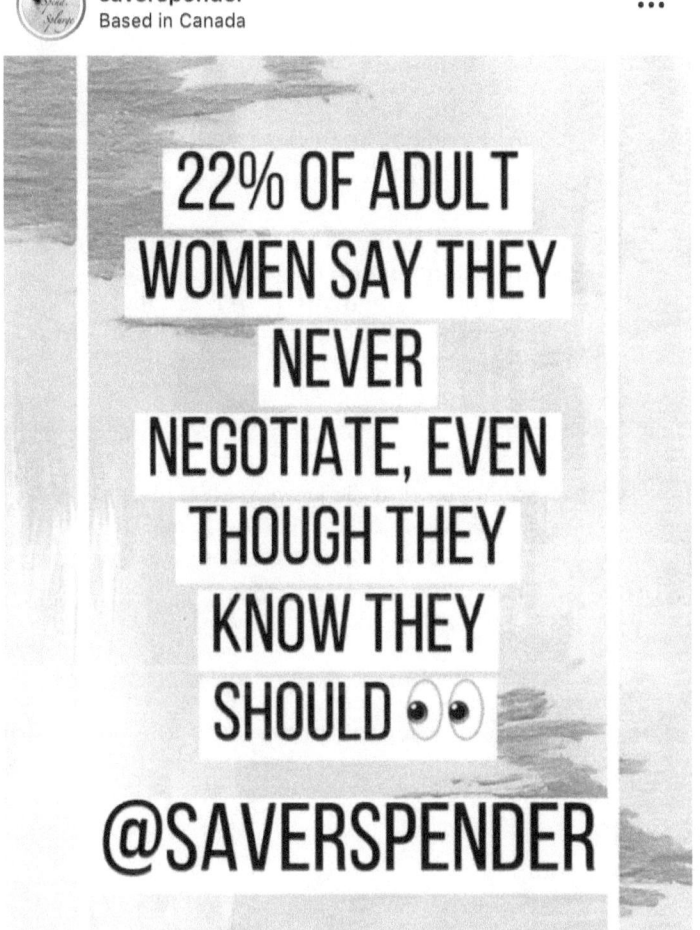

Then when someone posted a comment about their situation, I didn't just ignore it or like it, I responded back and started a conversation in the comments:

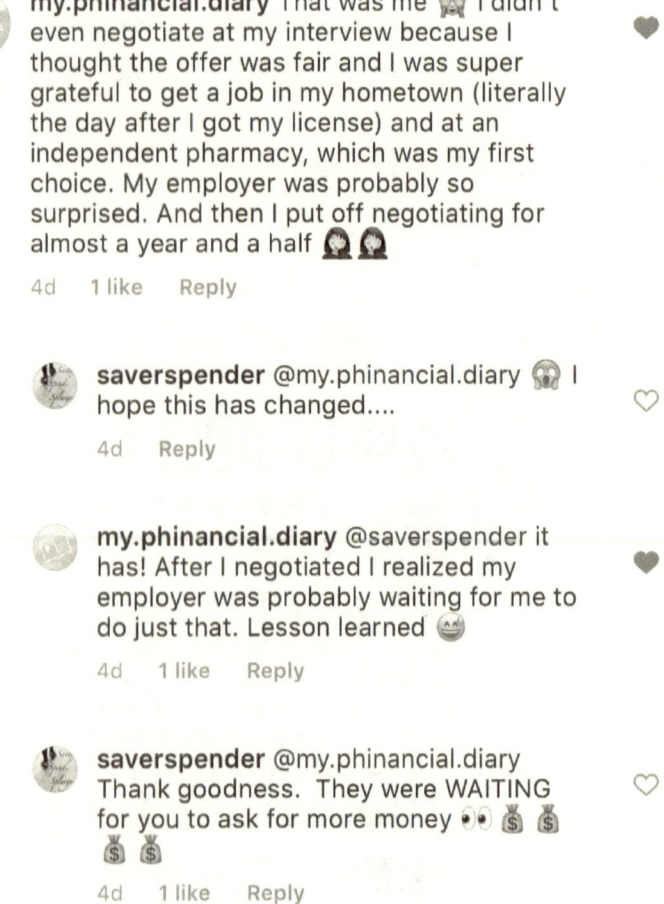

You would be surprised but other followers or people will go into your comments, and read other peoples' comments and/or like and continue the conversation!

So make it interesting. Every comment is an opportunity to engage more people and show your account off in its best light.

Leave Thoughtful Comments

Instead of just leaving simple single word or emoticon comments, leave something interesting.

Engage the person who wrote the post so that they write back, you have a witty repartee and they could hopefully want to go to your profile, and maybe get hooked / follow you back!

An interesting comment is not:

• Good job!
• Wow!
• Amazing!
• 💪

It is doing something like drawing them out with a question or asking for advice:

That's an incredible story. What would you say would be your best advice out of this whole situation?

Or you leave an actual, thoughtful comment about your own experience:

I went through something similar, and the best advice I can give is to stay calm and try not to focus on things you cannot control.

Feel free to add personal details, and a story that makes others who are curious, read your comment, like it, maybe reply to it, and come visit your profile. Think: What would YOU like to read?

Feature accounts you admire

If you feature them and genuinely enjoy their account, guess what?

They'll be flattered and may even repost, or at the very least, share it to their Stories which will give you some traction to their Followers.

I wouldn't say to do this all the time because you don't want to come off as though you're doing it just to get reposts or shares to a Story.

It also helps keep your account on the forefront of their mind - the more interactions you have with them, the more you stand out from the noise of the hundreds to thousands of comments and messages they may get in a day.

Please be careful with this strategy however; be choosy, be thoughtful, be genuine and don't force it just because they have a lot of followers.

You'd be surprised - a lot of accounts that had thousands of followers shared my account to their Stories but because of various reasons, they never sent more than maybe 5 followers.

Then others, who have had under 5000 followers shared my account, and I had a lot more followers come from them.

This happens for a few reasons:
• Your account doesn't vibe with their followers
• Their followers may not really watch their Stories
• It wasn't posted at the right/time/day/context
• Maybe they just happened to have an overload in their Stories that day and people just tapped right to get through to the end

Share Direct Messages for Promotion

I received this great message (so sweet!):

> I'm halfway through your book and I must admit.. I knew absolutely nothing about blogging except the writing part. Hahaha.. I'm so glad I'm reading this. There is so much to learn. Thanks

..and shared it on my Stories:

> I'm halfway through your book and I must admit.. I knew absolutely nothing about blogging except the writing part. Hahaha.. I'm so glad I'm reading this. There is so much to learn. Thanks

The income you see me make today on my blog is work I have done over 6 years to get to this point, but with a decade of experience.

I wrote this book "Start a Blog Like a Boss" on how to start a blog and shortcut all of my dumb, expensive mistakes including actual technical screenshots of how to set everything up from scratch.

Use Stories to keep your grid on brand

Anything I want to share that is personal, or maybe not "on brand" (e.g. parenting stories with Little Bun), I put in my Stories because I don't want my grid to be focused on anything but my core message.

I use Stories to add personality, share interesting links even if they have nothing to do with my IG, and to show that there is a real person behind the profile.

Use tags in your Stories

Did you know that you can use tags in your Stories?

You can hashtag up to 10 of them in your Stories and they have a slim chance of showing up in feeds when people browse, but it doesn't hurt to try!

CTA in Stories

You don't need 10K followers to get people to engage with you. Use every bit of arsenal you have in your toolkit to get messages coming in, and interested in engaging with you, even if it is just an emotion to your Story. A way I do that, is using Polls or asking for Questions like doing Ask Me Anythings (AMAs):

It's a simple poll, but it keeps them invested in your profile to keep coming back and giving opinions because everyone loves to tell you what they think - so let them! Encourage them to engage with you.

Then, when you post these, make sure to wait about 5-6 hours and then screenshot the responses and post it with a little comment.

Here's another example:

The secret to this is that it may seem silly, but people LOVE to be asked for their opinion, even randomly.

I have gotten so many direct messages (more interactions, yay!) from people replying to these polls to give more information, or background, and this not only generates more of a connection but it can also give me post/story ideas of what people might like to see.

How to screenshot a clean-looking image

Nothing looks messier than a screenshot of a Story that isn't clear, and is frankly, quite distracting.

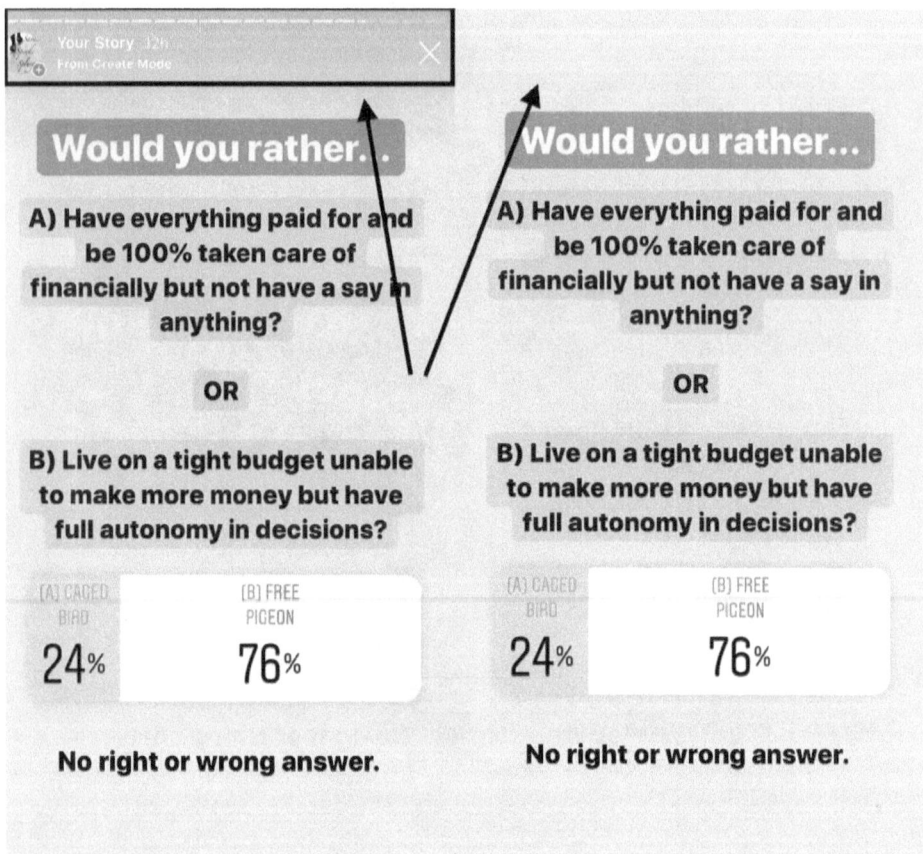

To screenshot a clean shot of the Story, hold down on the middle of the Story and wait for the header and footer to clear.

Then take the screenshot and you will see it looks much better without the header.

Send your post to your Stories

That way, people can easily tap on the post in your Stories, and go straight to the actual post itself to like and comment.

To do this, go to your Post and tap on the **Send** icon in the bottom left corner.

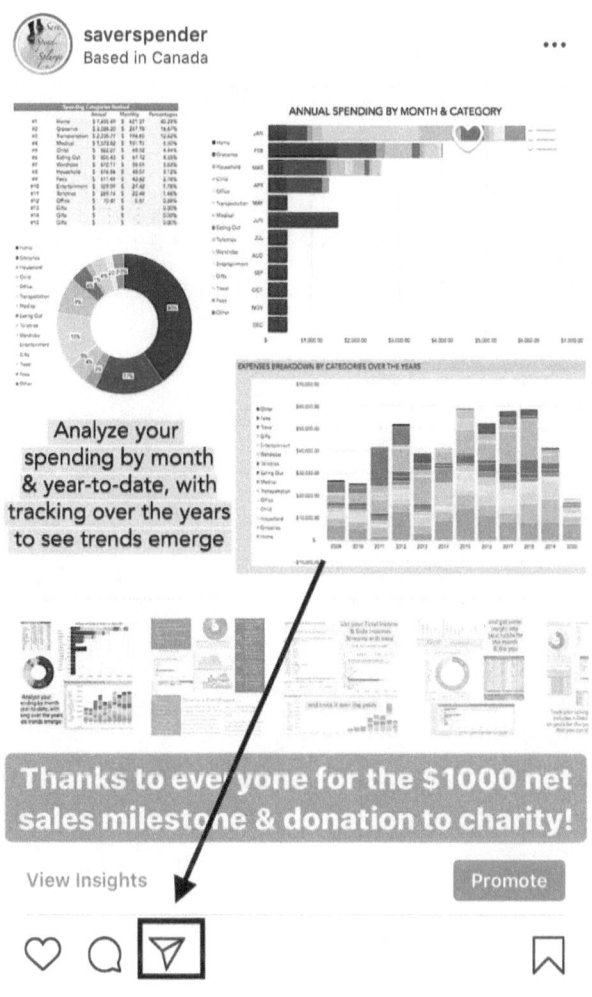

Now tap on **Add post to your Story**

Tip: You will also see a list of people you recently messaged just below this and you can send posts directly to others.

Sometimes I find and send posts to people who direct message me or leave a comment asking about something, and it helps add a personal touch to everything so they don't have to hunt through your posts to figure out what you're talking about.

Your Post in your Story will show up and can toggle between two looks, the first being very clean and the second with your IG handle and the first two lines of your caption.

To toggle back and forth, just tap in the middle of the post.

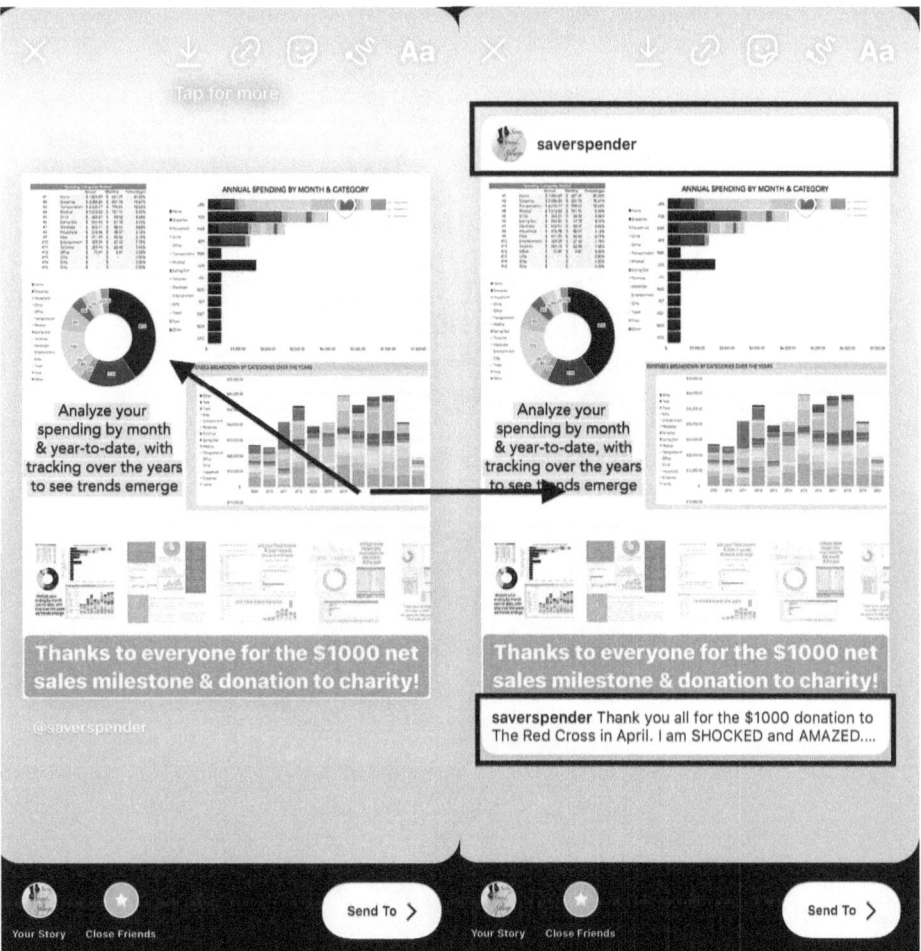

Which one you choose is up to you - sometimes you want your IG handle and a caption to help entice people to click on the post, and other times you just want to post the image.

Level up your 10K engagement

Don't let this magical superpower sit idly by. I use it every chance I get, even sending posts I created from my IG to my Stories, and adding the CTA link I put in the caption, in the Swipe Up itself!

Now, my Stories-followers, get to swipe up instead of having to click through hoops to read the post. This is another incentive for them to follow your Stories, and to keep it fresh with new content you don't post on your IG.

Use Stories as a testing ground

Sometimes I post ideas, or try out new things in my Stories as a testing ground for what people respond to. If you get interaction either a message, an emotion from what you posted, it means you have something there that you can expand on that is interesting.

The people who watch your Stories, is usually 10% of your followers and likely to be your strongest, most engaged core of followers.

They are the litmus test for the rest of your followers, and you want to do soft auditions of ideas, or ask them for feedback from time to time because they're on your side and rooting for you!

Some of my best posts have come out from things I shared, or typed in **Create** with ideas of what I wanted to talk about.

Observe what others are doing

Another good way to see what similar IG accounts (that you like) are doing, and observe their methods.

Some accounts are incredible at getting people to engage with them, and if you go through their Stories, their Posts, and read or pick up on what seems to make people comment, like or engage with them.

See what works for them - would it work for you? This is half of how I learned what to do because I thought - wow that looks fun and interactive, and then I did it.

Use Facebook Pages to manage interactions

IG has a major flaw where in your history, you may get a TON of activity of who liked, commented, or tagged you in things. As your profile grows, you will start missing out on all of these great interactions because *you simply don't see them any more.*

Enter: Facebook Pages (a secret tool for IG messaging) where all the **Comments** on your IG posts are stored:

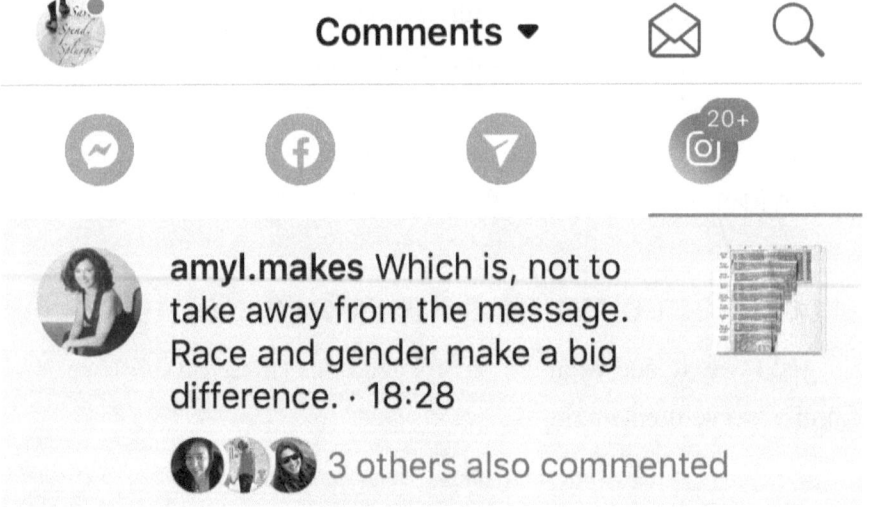

Now that Facebook owns IG, it makes it easier. If you have a Facebook Page set up for your IG Business/Creator account, and you can see the ENTIRE HISTORY of everything people have commented, or replied to your posts. You won't miss anything and you can take the time to go to each of your posts where some comments were missed/not replied to (even older posts), and respond back.

TOOLS

IG Bio Link

You absolutely need an IG bio link. Hands down, this is not optional.

You can obtain one from:

- Linktr.ee (Free) - https://linktr.ee/
- Tailwind (Smart.Bio) - https://www.tailwindapp.com/smartbio
- Later (Linkin.Bio) - https://later.com/linkinbio/
- Your own - You can create your own from your site & manually update it each time but this is quite time intensive

My Tailwind Smart.Bio looks like this as a link:

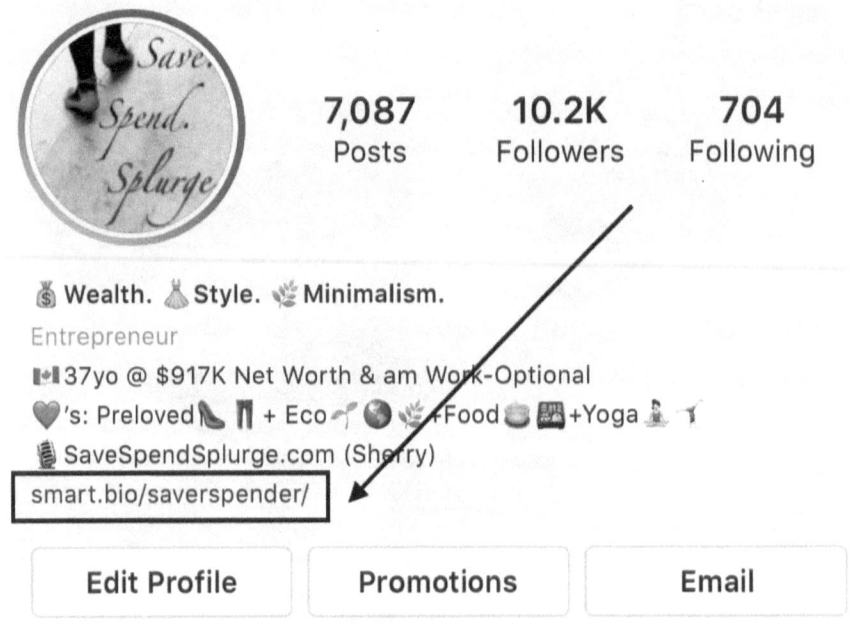

And you can see the bio has my major links at the top, and my new posts at the bottom:

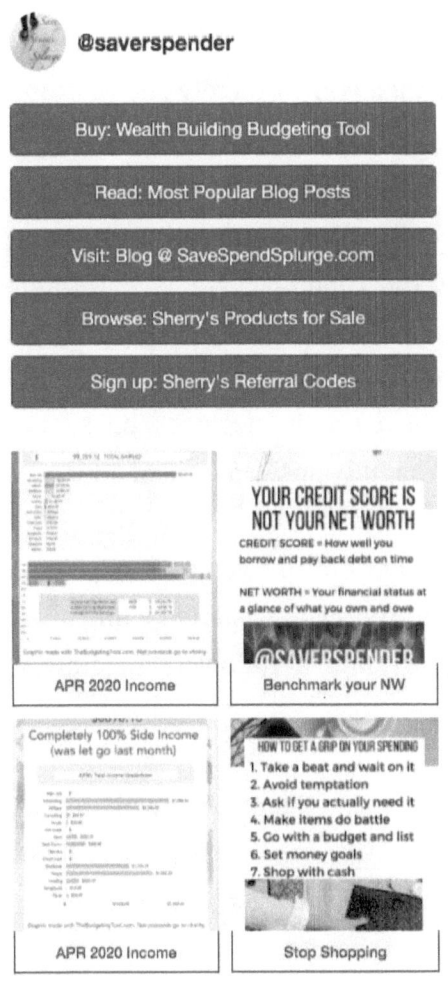

And it is like a mini starting page.

Third Party Scheduling
(Pinterest & Facebook)

If you are busy, and do not want to think about having to log in at the perfect time to post then you absolutely need a Third Party Social Media Scheduler.

There are two that are major players in this sphere and they are Tailwind (http://tailwindapp.com/) and Later (https://later.com/).

I personally use **Tailwind** and have been quite impressed with their customer service; I have sent in messages, bugs, questions, and they've always politely and happily answered/fixed a lot of my issues.

They also give out a lot of posts, webinars and ideas on how to grow your IG, but I can tell you from when I started with Tailwind versus what I was doing before, the uptick in followers is significant - I saw results almost within the week.

If you're interested in trying them out, my referral link is: (https://www.tailwindapp.com/i/saverspender) and you'll get 1 month free (and so will I but only if you decide their service is stellar and you buy the 1-year Plus program with them).

I pay $15 USD a month out of my pocket for them, and consider them my IG scheduling saviours and without them, hands down, I couldn't manage social media on my own as a one-woman band who also has a full-time family, sometimes career and blog to run. I use them to easily cross-post to Pinterest and Facebook.

Instagram (Facebook)

Don't want to pay for anything?

You can natively cross-post to Facebook via IG directly when you go to manually do the post as Facebook owns IG, so if you don't have Twitter or Tumblr, you won't need Tailwind for Facebook.

As for Pinterest, this is only useful to cross-post to, if you have a blog or a website to redirect people to.

I get a decent amount of trickle traffic to my blog from Pinterest from my posts on IG and it is worth the (very little) effort for me to schedule pins and create boards.

If you don't want to start up on Pinterest, at least focus on Instagram and cross-posting to Facebook and Twitter as the trio of social media platforms.

Just don't use Instagram for native posting to any platform BUT Facebook. Use Tweet.Photo for Twitter.

IFTTT (Tumblr)

As Tailwind doesn't let me also cross-post to Tumblr, I use a free applet service called IFTTT (https://ifttt.com/) for this.

The only applet I use in IFTTT is for **Tumblr**, but they do have other ones you can try out.

Caveat emptor - they all seem the same to me and only some work - so if you're willing to experiment go for it, but I got frustrated and gave up. The applet you want to look for is this one:

Keep your Tumblr fresh and up-to-date with your Instagrams. Note: only works for single photo posts.

Tweet.Photo (Twitter)

If you want to cross-post to Twitter, I recommend Tweet.Photo (https://tweet.photo/) and not Instagram natively. Do NOT post from IG because your tweets from IG show up like this when you post normally from IG:

What a waste right? No sexy IG image, nothing! Instead, if you use Tweet.Photo you get your full-sized IG image, and it does it automatically in the background with ZERO extra work!

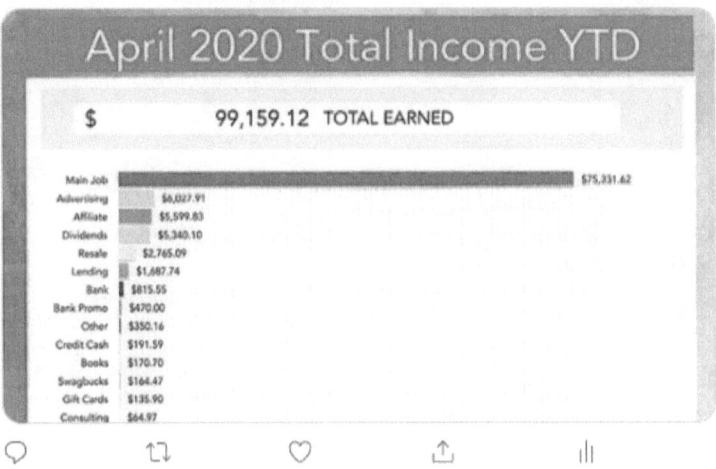

If you do this, you DO NOT need to tap cross-post to "**Twitter**" when you go to post manually. If you use Tailwind, this will not even be an issue, so it all happens in the background seamlessly and Tailwind won't post to Twitter either.

The only caveat that I'd say is you will see a tiny little blurb (as it is free) in the tweet that says **via tweet.photo** which for me is a small price to pay.

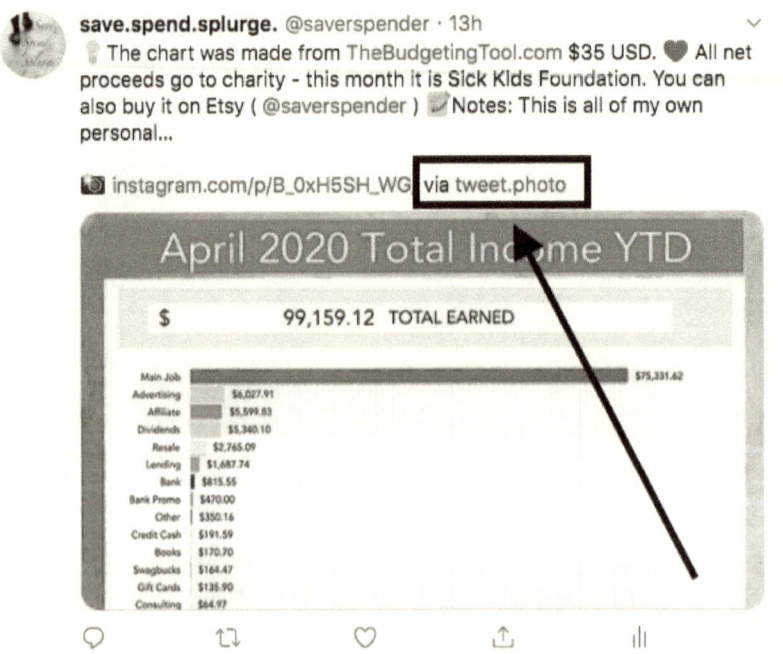

Unsplash Stock Photos

For free, beautiful, commercial-use and personal-use photos, use Unsplash (http://www.unsplash.com). They are my go-to stock photo provider and have beautiful images.

Search by any keyword you want like **Money** and you will see all the images with that keyword:

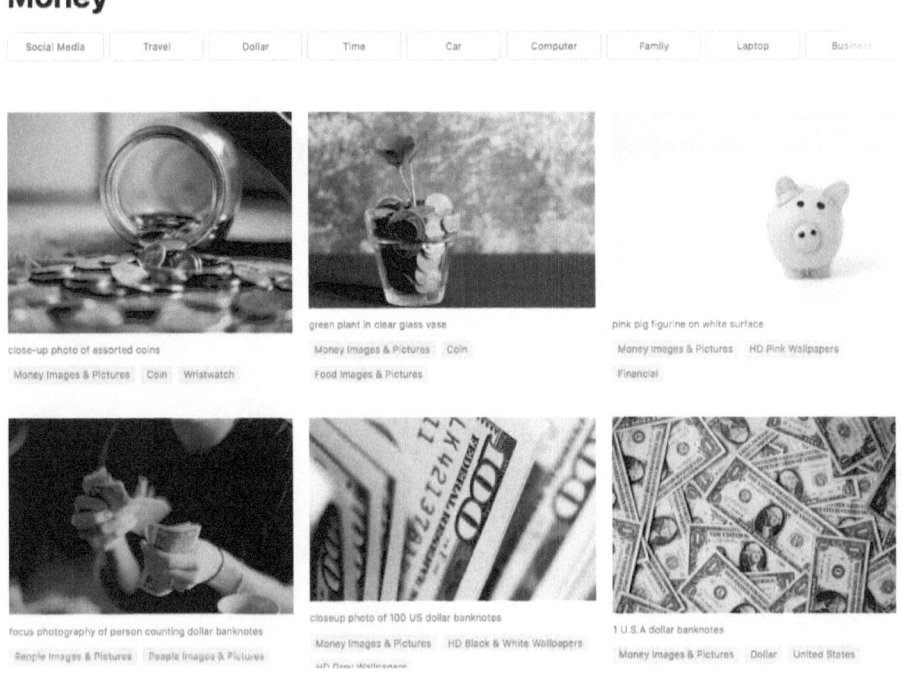

Image Editing Tools

If you want more customized photos, you will need some image editing tools. There are other ways to get around this with Unsplash stock photos and some creative usage of other tools I will get into, if you don't want to download and/or learn a new software. I'll cover all the methods below.

Your options are as follows:

Adobe Photoshop - $21 USD/month
https://www.adobe.com/products/photoshop.html
The holy grail of all editors, but very expensive.

Pixelmator - $30 USD
https://www.pixelmator.com/mac/
Great image editor for Mac OS systems that works perfectly for IG just as well as Adobe Photoshop

Paint.Net - $0
https://www.getpaint.net/download.html
Easy to learn image editor for the PC

GIMP - $0
https://www.gimp.org/downloads/
Image editor for Mac OS, PC or Linux

I would recommend buying an image editor and playing around with how to use it because they will pay themselves back over time but if you don't want to shell out for it, that's all right too, you will just need to spend more time tweaking things.

Image Edit with just your phone

If you want to avoid buying, downloading or learning any of the above, that's okay too.

You will need the following:
• Your phone
• Unsplash stock photos
• Image resizing app (e.g. Image Size)
• IG story creation app (e.g. Unfold)
• Instagram

WHY AN IMAGE RESIZING APP?

Your phone may not allow you to resize images to the maximum Portrait Mode required (Apple literally got rid of this option in their Photo app to remove the ratio resizing of 4:5 for Portrait mode in their last update and I got sick of trying to guess).

I use an iPhone, so the app I use is **Image Size** (https://apps.apple.com/au/app/image-size/id670766542) and it costs $6 USD to remove the ads (I paid for it because I got annoyed), but you can use it for free.

Image Size 4+
Resize your photo! Resizer App
Vitalij Schaefer

★★★★★ 4.6, 965 Ratings

Free · Offers In-App Purchases

Whatever you use, just make sure you have something that can easily resize down your image to the proper dimensions for **Portrait** mode.

Why an IG Story Creation app?
You can make beautiful looking posts without much work and the trick is to use IG Story Creation apps and then resize the images down once you're done.

I use **Unfold** (https://unfold.com/) and they're $0 (unless you want to pay to upgrade to their other templates and fonts), and are available for the iOS and Android.

I haven't bothered upgrading this one because I think what they have for free is fine, but you can decide for yourself.

Other Story Creation Apps

There is a range of free and paid apps or partially-free apps:

- Over (https://www.madewithover.com/)
- Storyluxe (https://apps.apple.com/app/apple-store/id1324447436)
- Canva (https://www.canva.com/)
- Piktochart (https://piktochart.com/) - Good for Infographics

METHOD 1: Add text to an image

1. Use your photo/find one on Unsplash

You can use Unsplash or you can also use an image of your own making (a screenshot, a picture). Download it to your phone.

2. Open it in IG and add text, etc

Add text, stickers, etc in IG then download the finished product as an image

3. Download the image at the top

This will save the finished image to your phone in your Photo/Images roll. Now, obviously it isn't at the right size that you need it to be (Portrait), so you need to resize it.

4. Resize it to be Portrait mode

Make sure your Width and Height are set to the following settings with Width = 1080 and Height = 1350.

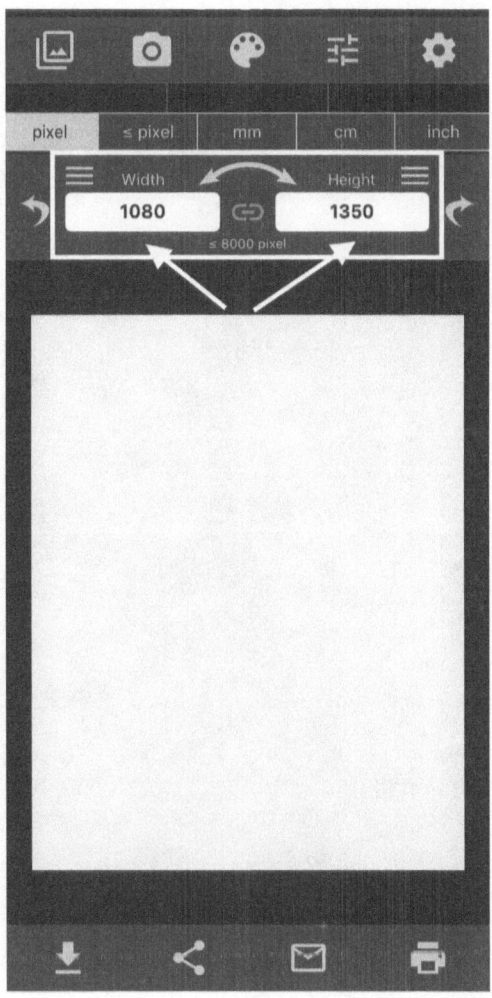

 If you don't play around with the settings, you can just leave it as-is and save a lot of time by just going into the app, choosing the image and resizing it quickly each time you need it.

Et voilà. A simply created image from your phone with text, resized for optimal Portrait mode to post.

You can just download it here with the arrow in the bottom left:

METHOD 2: Fancier image and text

Let's say you want something prettier - time to put in a little extra work on your phone if you don't want to use an image editing program.

1. Use your photo/find one

2. Craft a Story post using Unfold

Remember that you aren't posting in a Story, and a chunk of the entire image will get taken out when you resize it, so try and keep the content to the middle. First, start a new Story Template:

Now you need to choose a template that has text in the middle (if you want to write something); you can see a whole bunch of different options and anything with a blue dot means it needs to be an in-app extra purchase of other template sets:

Now fill in the template with text, images, and what you want to see on a post:

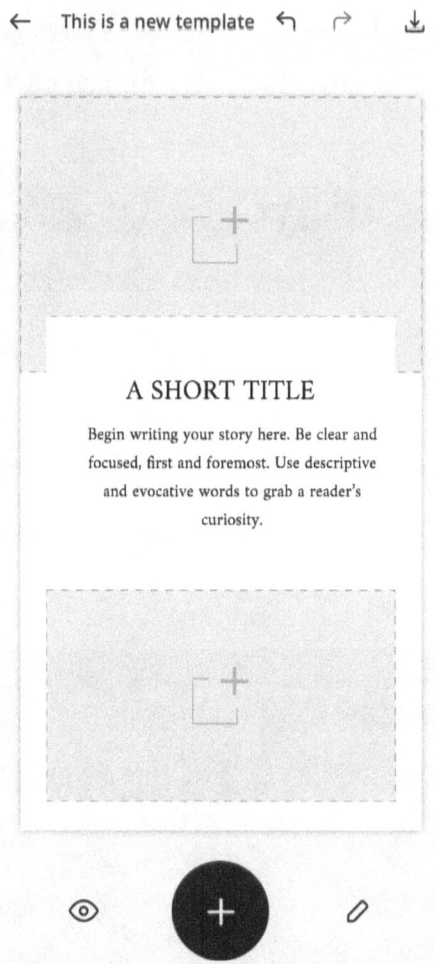

You can add a title in the middle, text in the bottom, change the font, the size, the colour, etc.

You cannot however, add a background to the text which I find really limiting, but I will show you a little trick for that after this.

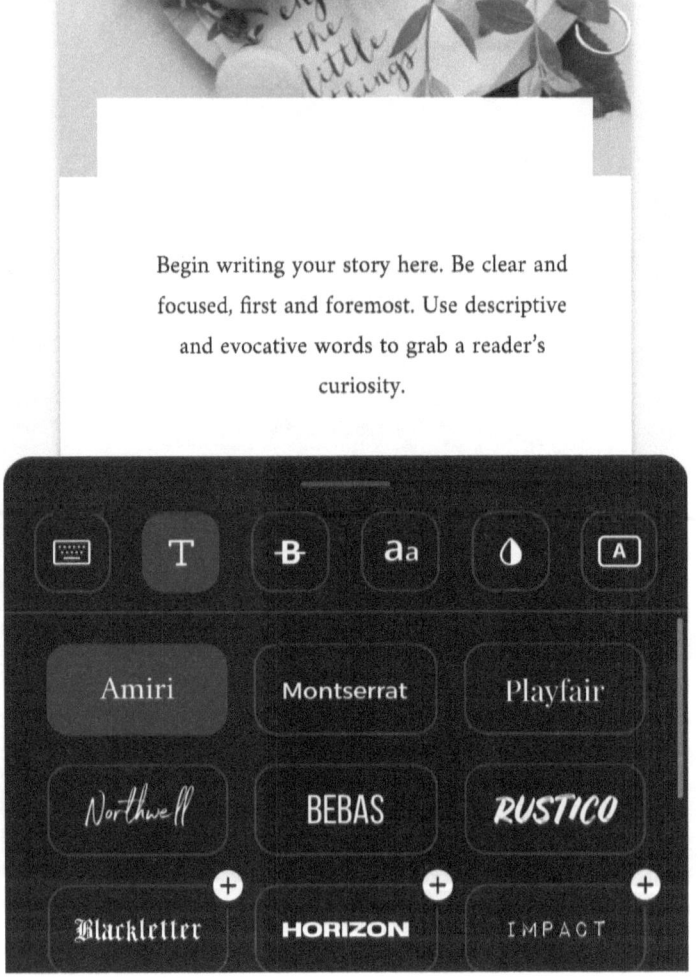

Anything with a + also is an extra in-app purchase if you want those fonts. I have just stuck with the free fonts.

You can also add extra text, stickers or other new things to the Story itself with that little pencil in the bottom right corner.

3. Download the image at the bottom to save it to your Image Roll

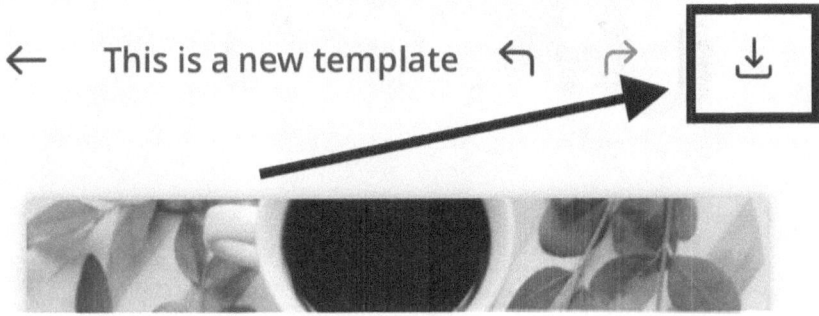

4. Resize it

And now you have a beautiful Post that will be in Portrait mode and ready to post just as it is.

This is the body of the text.
Type as much as you want
but remember that the
font has to be big enough
to see on a phone clearly.

TIP! Need to remember when posting Portrait Sized photos in IG

If you aren't using a Third-Party scheduling app, you will need to press on the bottom right section to 'widen' the image so it posts in Portrait mode and lengthens the image.

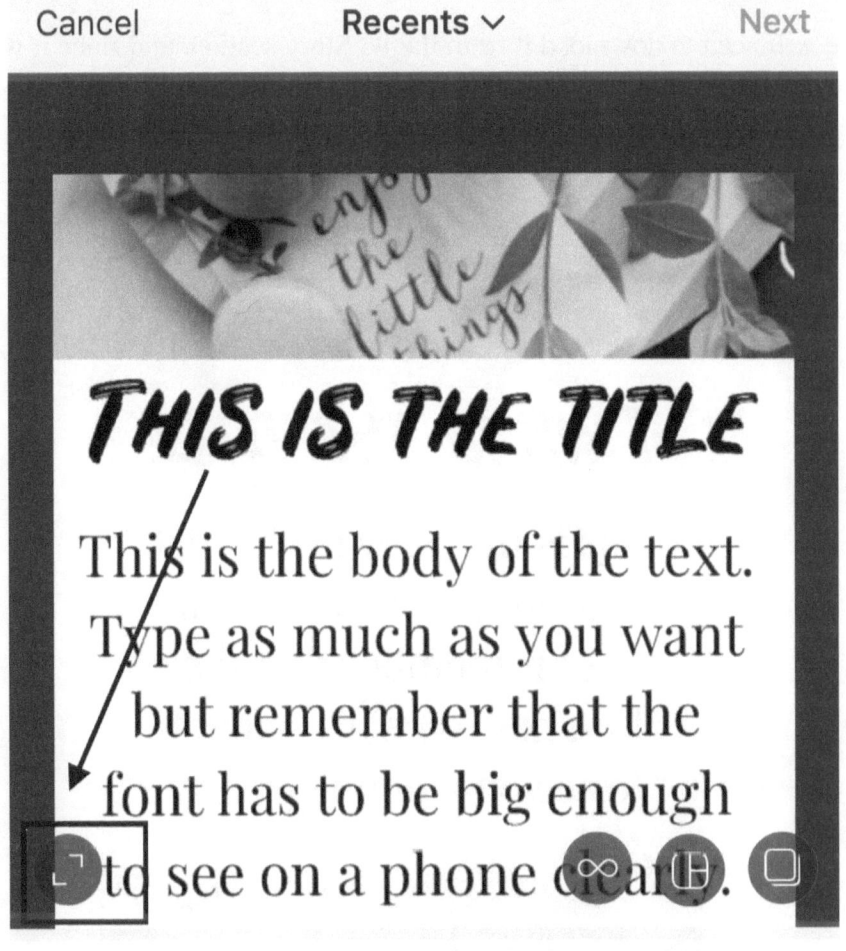

TIP! Add text like your IG Handle in IG's Stories if need be

I sometimes take the **Unfold** final result and add my tag in IG because I find the font there bolder and easier to read, and you can put any colour background to the text to make it stand out. In Unfold it doesn't give you that option to put a background on your text.

You will need to download it from the IG Story section, and since it will download the whole Story including the tops and bottoms, you will need to resize it again.

This is the body of the text.
Type as much as you want
but remember that the
font has to be big enough
to see on a phone clearly.

TIP! Use stickers in Unfold as a background instead

So this takes a little more finesse but can look very cool if you are patient with steady fingers. Go into Unfold, and add a sticker to use it as a background (only the first 2 are free, the rest with the + are in-app purchases):

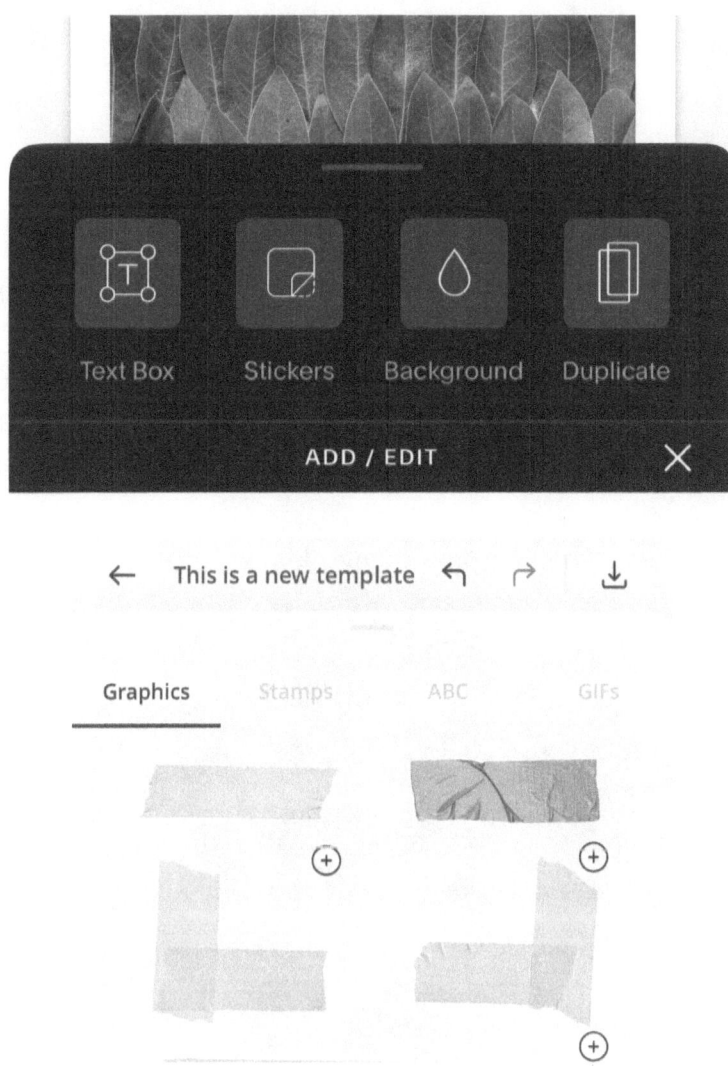

Select the Sticker that you want, and resize it to make it bigger:

And then add another Text box on top of it with your image:

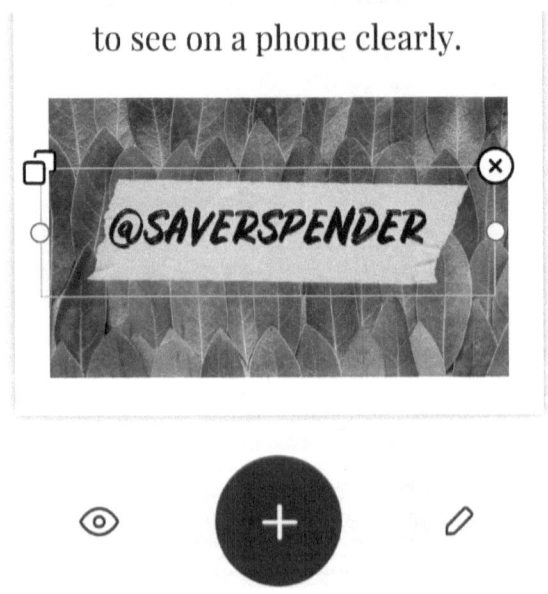

The only finicky thing is that these are layers and if you tap on the sticker by accident, the text disappears behind it, and you have to re-shift everything around again. (You may swear a lot, I'm warning you.)

When done right, it can look killer though, check out what I did here for a Story as part of an Introduction to myself when I hit 10K followers:

Layout (Make mosaics)

Another app you can use to simply smash together some images, is **Layout from Instagram**.

Layout from Instagram 4+
Instagram, Inc.
#13 in Photo & Video
★★★★★ 4.4, 6.6K Ratings

Free

It is easy to use, but the only downfall between using this and the **Unfold** app, is that it only creates images in Square, not Portrait mode. Still, it can be useful for images like this when you want to post multiples:

Create video posts

Apps that help you do this are **Boomerang from Instagram** and **Mojo** (https://mojo.video/) both available on iOS and Android.

If you post videos in your Story, it has to be under 15 seconds or else it creates a second video (they split them into multiple sides).

You also cannot select multiple video files of longer-than-15-second lengths because it will only take the first video and not the rest of the videos (I have tried).

You can also be creative and use Screen Recording on your phone.

• Tap on Screen Recording on your phone (on iOS swipe down from top)
• Open up your Notepad app
• Start typing the post you want
• Resize it on your phone to be Square
• Post it as a video post of you... typing!

It takes a bit of practice and work (I suggest writing the script out beforehand), because with fat fingers, you can accidentally have typos and have to redo the entire Screen Recording over again.

OTHER

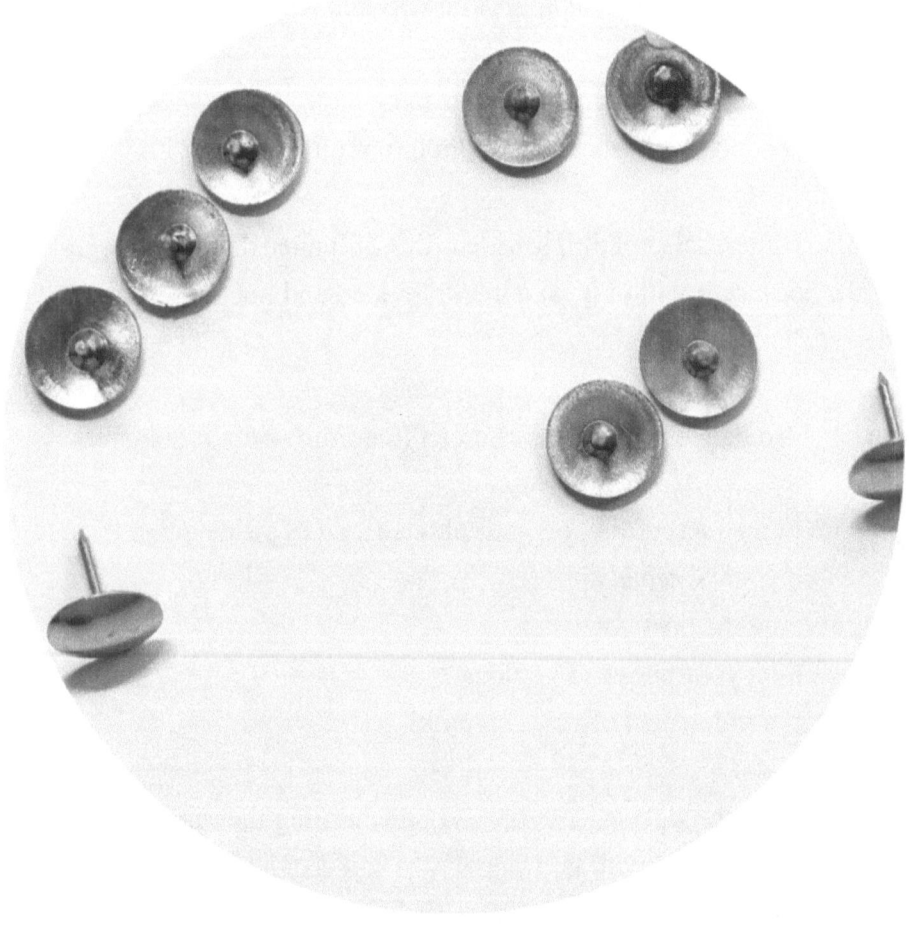

Highlights

You will want to have highlights in your profile. No more than 6 highlights or less because people will get fatigued if they're scrolling constantly. My old highlights were a little messy (I had 10!), and all over the place in terms of subject, not necessarily pertaining to the page:

I concentrated them down to 5 highlights and tried to put the focus on my products and books along with the key messages for my IG and blog:

Now they look cleaner, and have a sort of running theme of black and white and high heels (all images from Unsplash).

Remember that on a phone, you're going to see even less, at best 4 full ones and even the 6 I see on the desktop above, look like this on my phone:

How to set highlight covers without spamming

To easily set highlight covers without spamming people with your Stories of the images you want to show.

1. Have your Highlight Cover images ready on your phone.

2. Click on your **Profile** then the **Highlight** you want to change

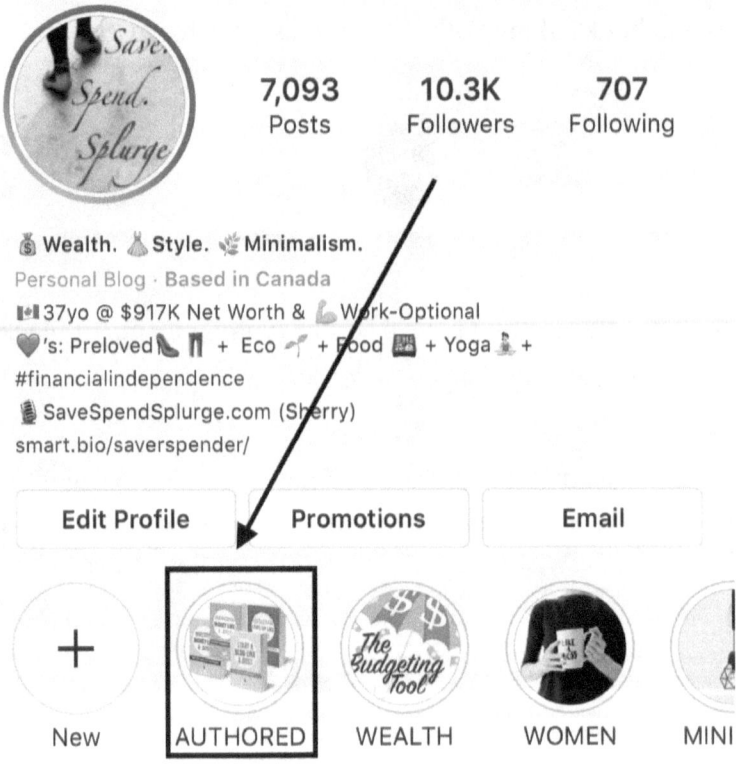

3. You will see the first Highlight, click on the bottom right corner with the 3 dots and **More** to edit it

4. Click on **Edit Highlight**

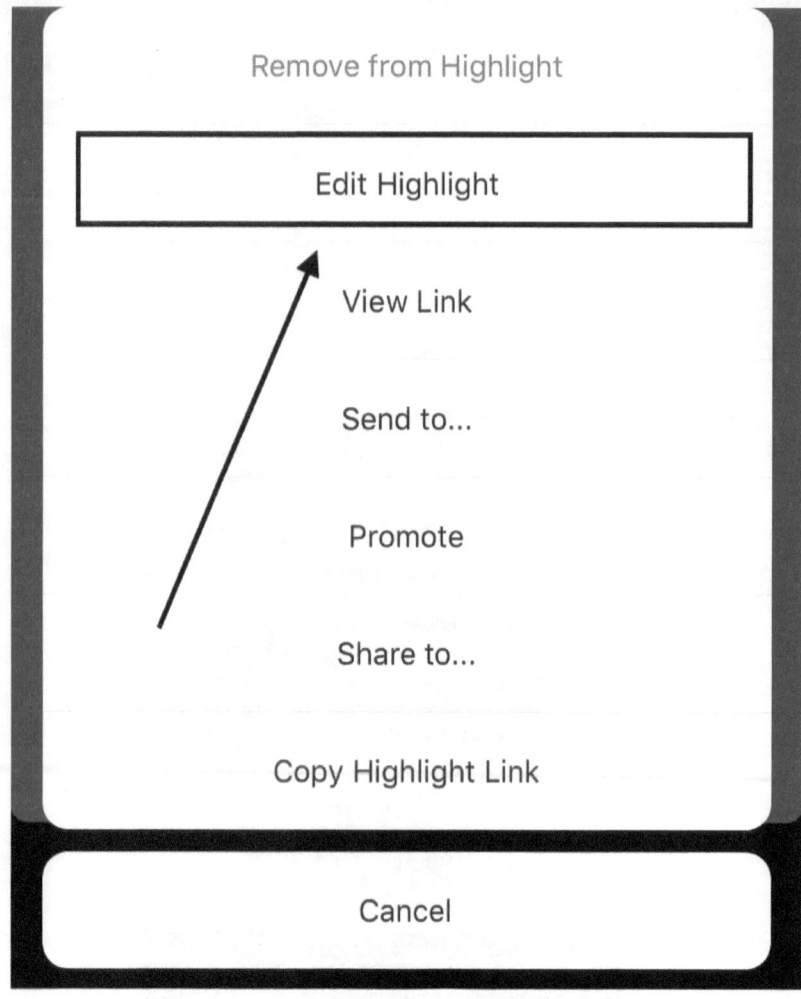

Name   AUTHORED

5. Click **Edit Cover**

6. Click on the **Image** icon to the far left

7. Select your image and arrange it in the circle and you're done!

Cancel   Recents ˅   Done

Note: The resolution on these images don't have to be amazing because they're going to be tiny little highlight cover images, but if you're a stickler for details, the maximum sizing is: 1080 x 1920 pixels as a size.

Create Highlight Covers in Stories

You can also use IG to create the Highlight Covers by creating the images in there.

Open up your IG Stories, choose a colourful background or a solid coloured one, and type some text, then download it as an image that you can then use.

Highlight Cover Ideas

You can use custom covers you've created, Unsplash photos, solid colours, or even solid colours in a monochromatic gradient, icons, etc. You can also get creative with the name (it does cut off at 7 characters when you're doing ALL CAPS or 10 characters with lowercase letters).

Think about using emoticons in there as well, or create the names with just dots to keep it minimalist. Here are some Highlight Covers & Names, with some commentary:

Jewelry Necessaire Eats Home Blog Posts Etsy Favs Quarantine

These highlights are fine, but they aren't eye-catching for me (a little busy) and not very cohesive, but the names are clear & kind of cute ("necessaire")

SHOP WORDS REPOST WALLPAP... ANSWERS POSITIVITY BULGARIA

Here she is highlighting her work as an artist which is a great idea; but note how the word "WALLPAP…" cuts off?

Snowflake... Project 333 Frugal me... Intro & Debt Closet

You could create some custom icons against bold coloured backgrounds.

Keep it fun and minimal with just words and dots as the names, although I will say I personally find this highlight cover font difficult to read and I don't like squinting.

Or how about just all one colour (simple!) with words below?

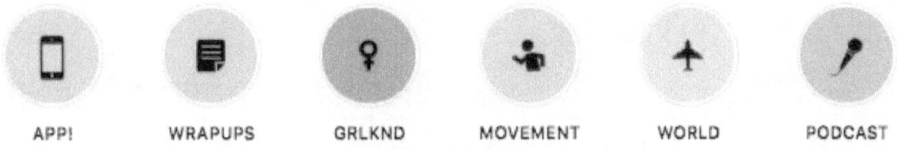

You could also make these solid colours monochromatic in one tone or shade, going from light to dark, based on your branding with an icon.

Or try a trio of colours from your brand.

Free Print ...   Courses   Foundrv1....   Epic Blog ...   Success S...   Digital Mag   Foundr Po...

Or how about bright red background with a mix of images & icons?

Ask the Pr...   Tips   Growth   Product   Sales   Marketing   Tech

Another idea would be having the icons in a circle to make the highlights stand out.

TRAVEL   BLOG   SHOP

For the Highlight name, why not space it out? Instead of **TRAVEL** type it as **T R A V E L** to give it some emphasis

Consider using emoticons by themselves, or with words to add interest.

Play around with all, or some of these ideas, and see what looks best to you and for your brand.

Little IG Tips and Tricks

I am assuming you know how to use IG on a basic level, but if you want to know some fun Story tips and design tricks, here are some things I found very useful.

1. Make an entire IG story background be a full colour

In **Create** mode, now tap on **Aa** on the bottom to move on to the next section:

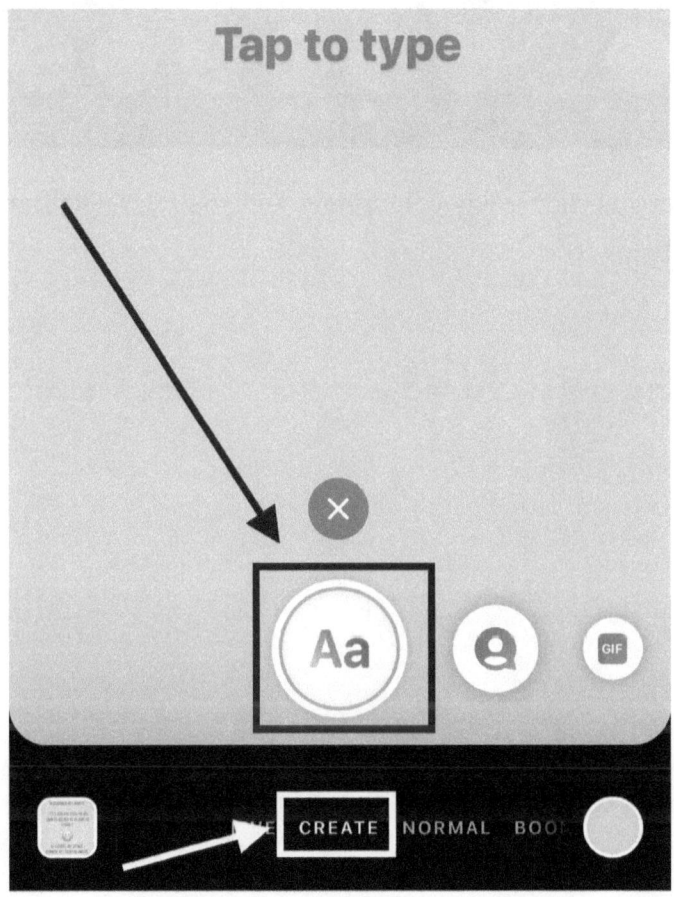

Select the **Marker** icon:

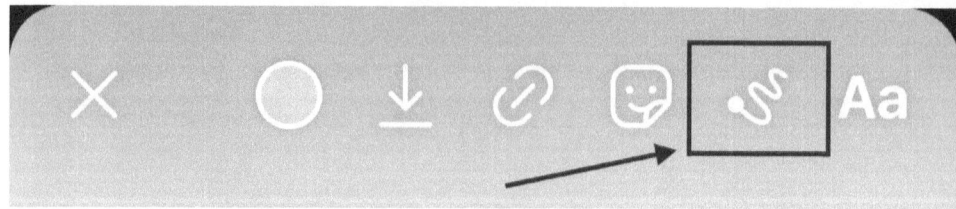

Now select the **Eyedropper**:

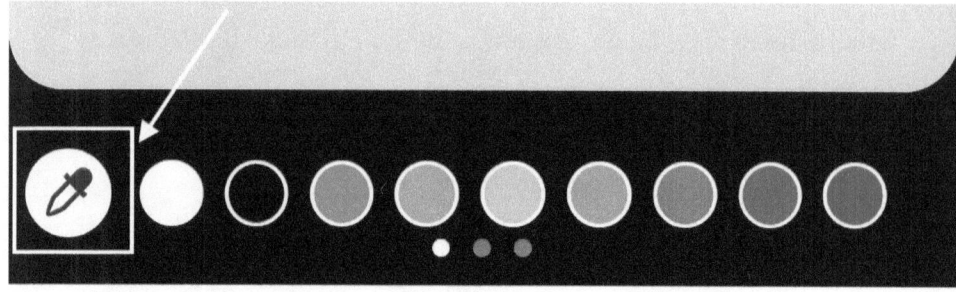

That will let you choose any colour now, and you can select from the row of colours below:

So let's say I want this pale pink colour:

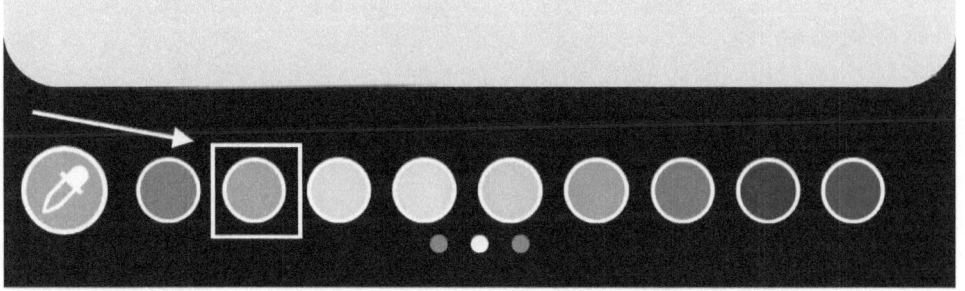

Now hold on to the screen with your finger for 2 seconds and the entire background will change:

2. Create pops of colour behind text

Type something:

Now use **Marker** to colour behind the **Text**:

3. Create eraser cutouts on images

You must select an image to use the background. You can do a picture too.

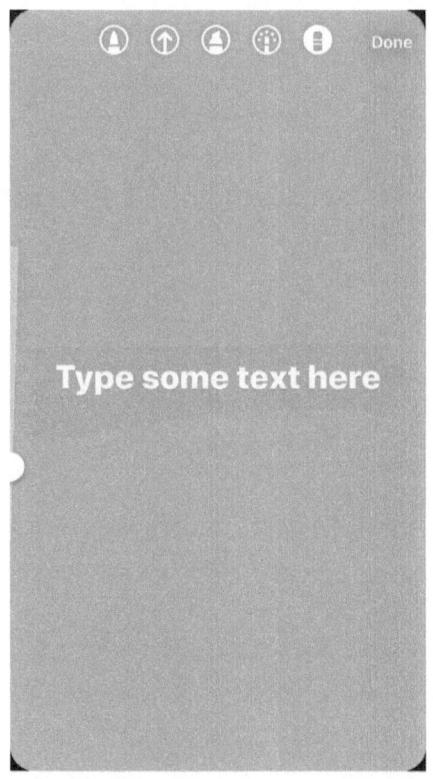

Now tap on **Marker** and if you want to (or not), select a colour (or else the default is light grey):

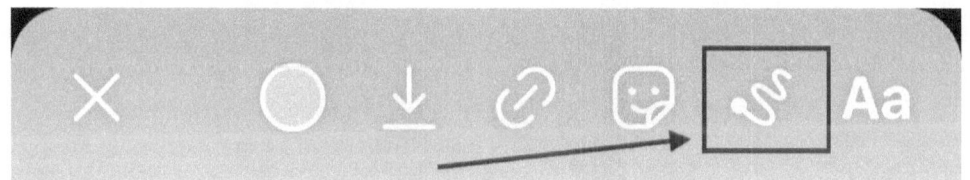

Make sure the Marker is selected and then hold down on the screen to cover it in a layer of light grey:

Now tap on the **Eraser** icon

And erase parts of it to "reveal" what is underneath; depending on how big you want the circles to be, adjust the size of the Eraser marker:

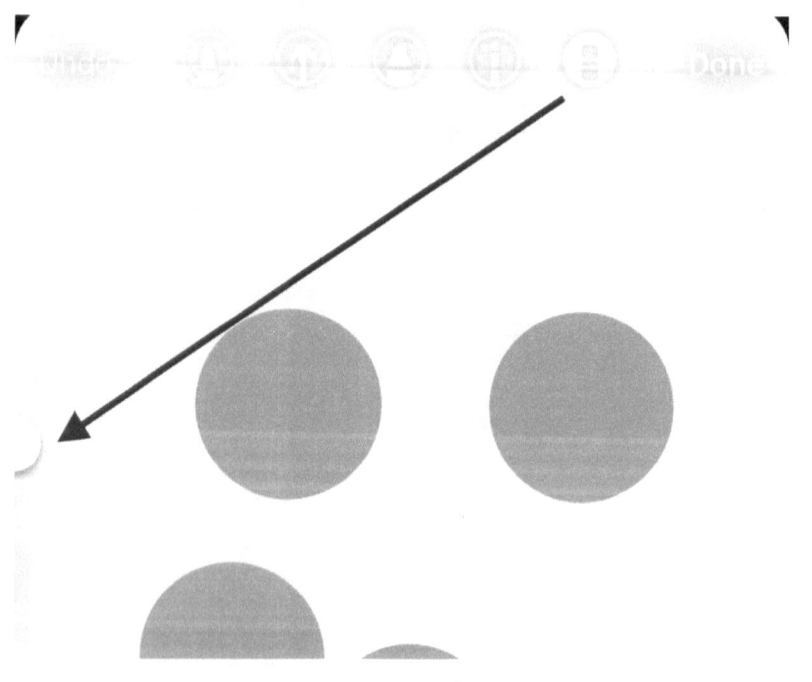

4. Choose a colour palette for your Stories

I don't do this, but you could always stay "on brand" and choose a colour palette for your Stories that you always use, so that when someone taps over to your Stories they know INSTANTLY it is your brand.

5. Share a lot more on your Stories than Posts but keep it cool

Sharing a lot on your Stories, at least 5-10 times a day has done my account a lot of good because each time you share a Story, your account shifts to the top of the Story Line and stays in the forefront of people's IG accounts.

They all disappear after 24 hours anyway.

I've noticed the Stories I watch the most, are from people who post the most often and therefore, are at the top of my IG feed and at strategic times when people are most likely to be browsing on IG (not at midnight for instance).

That said, don't go overboard with this.

Having a set of Stories be little tiny dots at the top can be overwhelming because it's like having a full Inbox of emails.

Would you rather read only 5 emails or 500?

People will tap right just to get through them unless they're super dedicated followers.

Stories are the same.

Hide your Story from Specific Users

Not sure why you would do this but if it ever comes in handy, you can hide your Stories from specific users (maybe if you're trying to surprise them?). Go to that User's Profile and click on the 3 dots in the top right corner:

Now select **Hide Your Story**

Analyze your Spikes

You really need to post and check each post to see how it is doing. Some will go gangbusters and you have no idea why, and others you thought would be gems, will flop. You have to learn what works for YOU.

50% of that is timing

You have to know the right times when people are engaged and actually scrolling through IG.

Remember - IG has an algorithm that determines who gets to see your post.

If you post something at 6 a.m. when people are not as engaged, versus at 5 p.m. when they are, you are going to obviously get more eyeballs on your post.

50% of that is content

You have to create content that is itching to be shared; either something funny, informative, or personal.

It sounds so glib to say: "Well, post good content!" … but that's what you have to do. You need to find your vibe and what works for you, your page, and your style - you need to be authentic to your brand and honest.

Don't post what you think other people want. Post what you think you want to see, otherwise you will not post anything worth looking at or sharing.

How Instagram works in 2020

It used to be your posts were shown to 10% of your followers but they have been tweaking it a lot and it relies on 6 things:

1. Relationship
2. Interest
3. Real-Time
4. Frequency
5. Following
6. Usage

RELATIONSHIP

If you like, watch the Stories of, comment on, and talk to an account more often, you will see more of their posts. This is a great thing because it means you need to get people to consistently interact with your account, and it means you will hold a stronger relationship with them as a result.

INTEREST

Based on what you are following, sometimes you may have seen that IG will say: **"You liked X amount of posts this week with this hashtag! Do you want to follow?"** .. or something along those lines. This means the more you enjoyed a post with those hashtags, or from that IG account, the higher it will appear on your feed. The likes that people are leaving and comments, will mean their posts will show up more often for you.

As IG is slowly getting rid of Likes or at least showing the number of likes, it means you need to get people to engage with you and comment on your IG account to keep that interest going.

Comments will be the big thing, and getting people to want to say something about what you've written will be crucial. No more skating by with just likes.

REAL-TIME

The newer posts show up higher on people's feeds. This absolutely does NOT mean you need to post like crazy, but you do need to post when people are most likely to be on so they can see your post, like it and COMMENT.

FREQUENCY

Each time someone opens the IG app, the best posts of that time that are 'trending' will appear on top of the list, even if they are 2 hours old, or 6 hours old and not 2 minutes old.

FOLLOWING

The more accounts you follow, the more work IG has to do to sort through all of them. The less you follow, the more posts you'll see from each user.

This one is tricky because I like to follow a wide range of accounts, and I've also noticed that if I follow accounts similar to mine, I am more likely to show up on the **"Suggested Accounts for you"** section for new followers I might have otherwise not reached, had I not followed an account and 'tapped' into their base of followers.

Personally though, I love that the less you follow, the more you will see from them (I miss so many posts). Professionally, you might want to consider following at least within your inner circle of accounts you want to be associated with. Their followers are likely to want to follow you as well, if you write similarly.

USAGE

How much time you spend on IG determines how much data they have to work with, so if you are only there for 10 minutes, IG will only show you the best posts. If you stay on there and spend more than 10 minutes, you'll see way more content in general because there's more time to cull data and show you other / older posts.

I've noticed this when I scroll through IG (I am on there a lot), and I see that there are posts from 6 hours ago, and after I scroll past those 'highlights', I end up getting into posts that weren't doing as well.

Again, how much interaction you get on each post - Likes (for now) and Comments, Shared to Stories, Sent To Others, are what determines whether or not IG considers your post a "popular post" that people like.

The more people who interact (and not just like) with your account via comments and so on, the more IG thinks you're popular enough to show others as a Highlight.

I've done experiments where I have posted things I KNOW will do well and I save these posts strategically for a time when I know lots of people are on (typically between 6 p.m. and 10 p.m. EST), and if within the first 10 minutes I get a lot of likes, I know it will end up being a Highlight Post on others' feeds when they open IG.

Sample Posting Schedule

You absolutely do not need to follow this, but here is a sample posting schedule I follow:

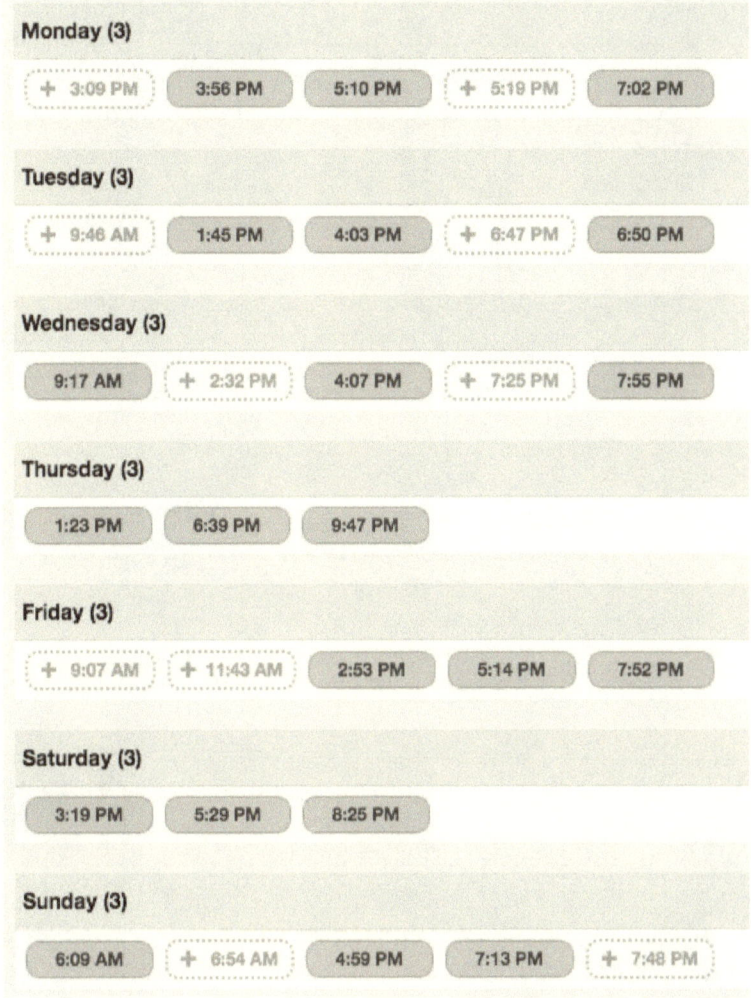

I try to post at least 3 - 4X a day. You can choose to post less than that as long as you are CONSISTENT.

I always try and hit the highlighted green blocks, and if (rare) there is a 4th post I want to do for a day I think more people are engaged because I happen to have a one-off post (e.g. Re-Introduction Post, Re-Introduction of all of my Books), I'll do it.

Decode your Post Insights

For instance, I look at some posts that do well and here's how you can analyze what happened.

What each icon means (going from left to right, top to bottom):

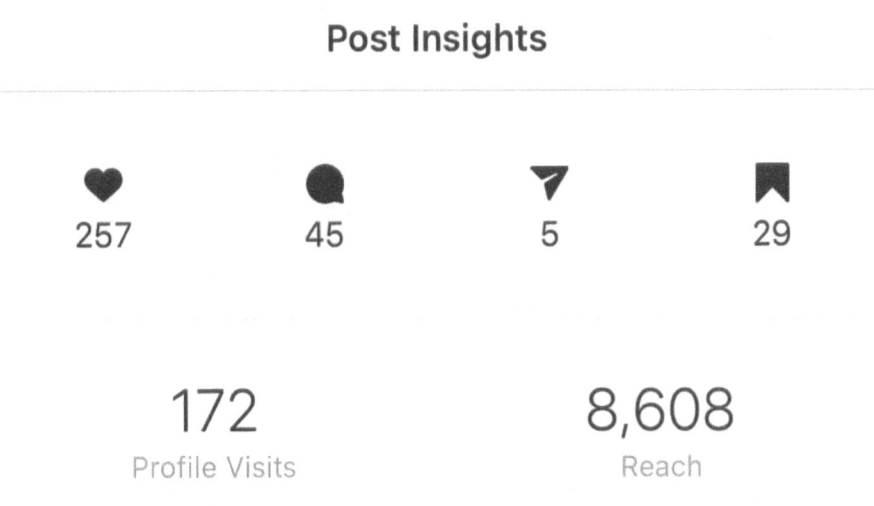

- Likes = 257 likes
- Comments = 45 interactions
- Sent Post = 5 people thought enough of it to share it with others
- Bookmarked = 29 people wanted to save it for later
- Profile Visits — 172 people came to the profile (and hopefully Followed)
- Reach = 8608 eyeballs on the post

What each icon will mean for you:

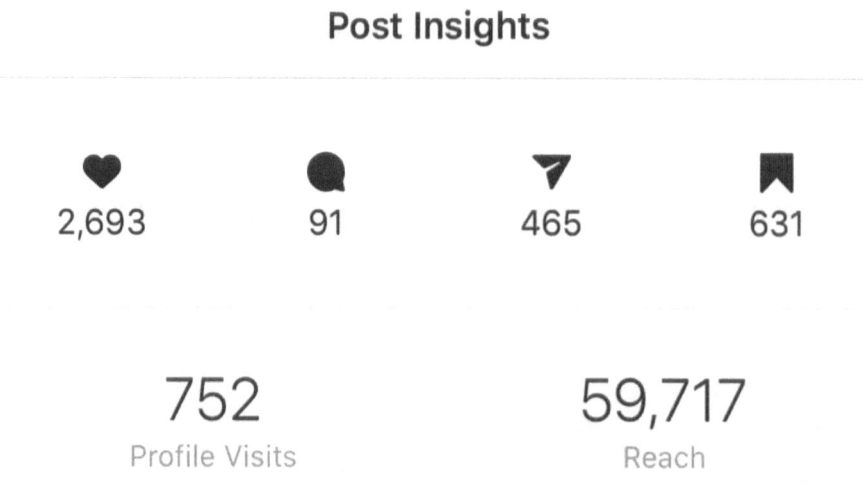

Post Insights

❤	💬	➤	🔖
2,693	91	465	631

752
Profile Visits

59,717
Reach

The **Likes** are what make IG want to show the post to more people and keep it higher up in the feed of people who are browsing your 30 hashtags, which helps with **Reach**.

The **Comments** mean that people are engaged and interested which is good for your own personal IG growth.

The **Sent Post** is THE most important metric for sharing and helps get even more people interested in your post, like it, and maybe comment (it just boosts overall IG participation and boosts your profile to more people).

The **Bookmarked** is important to know that people wanted to keep it enough to save it.

Every post that goes out, has to be analyzed with **Insights** and **Analytics** to see why it did well.

What to pay attention to when you see a post spike:
- Time you posted
- Day you posted
- Hashtags used on the post
- If anyone shared your post - obviously reciprocate and engage!
- What you posted - the content, topic, or angle - could it be something you can replicate again or post similar content on?

Decode your Profile Insights

Click in the top right of your Instagram profile to access the **Menu**:

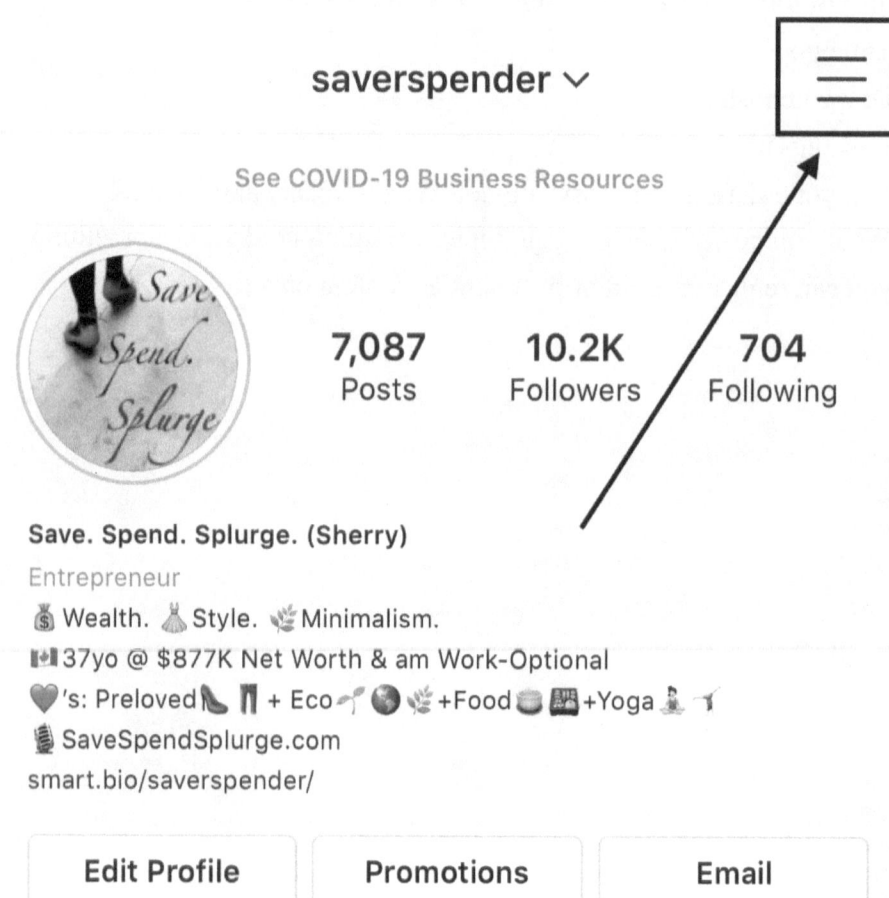

Click on **Insights**:

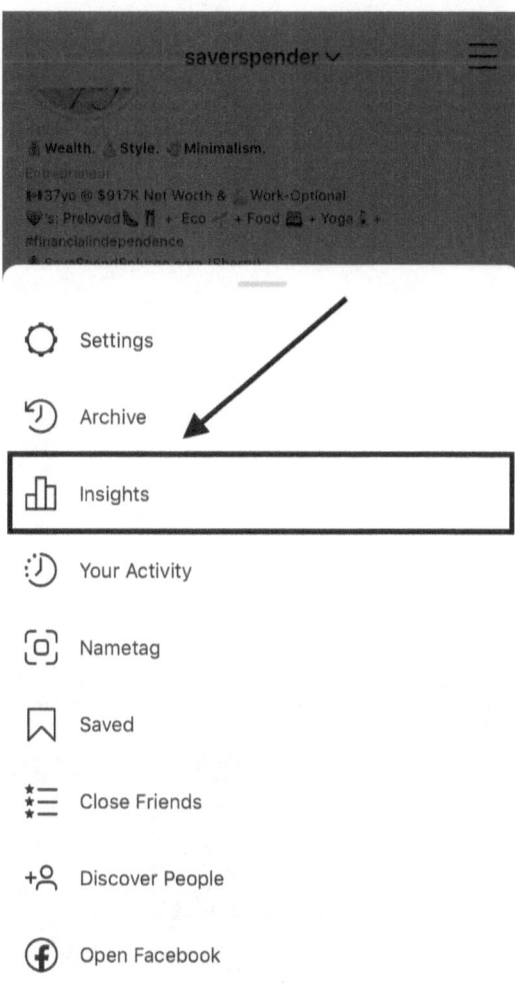

You can see which posts have done well so far:

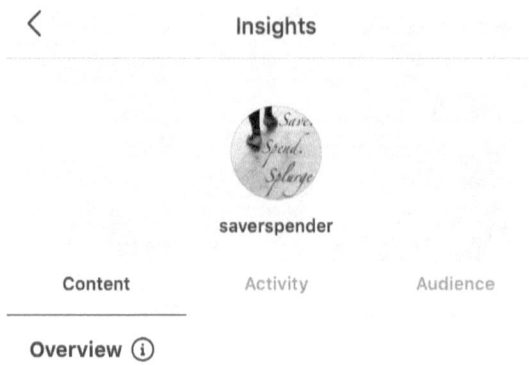

Insights

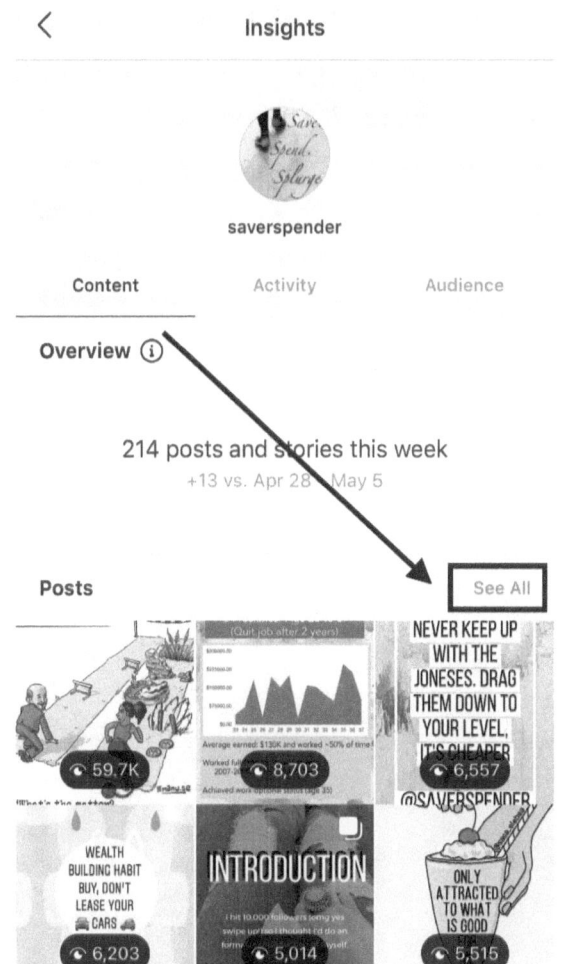

From here, you can select Time period:

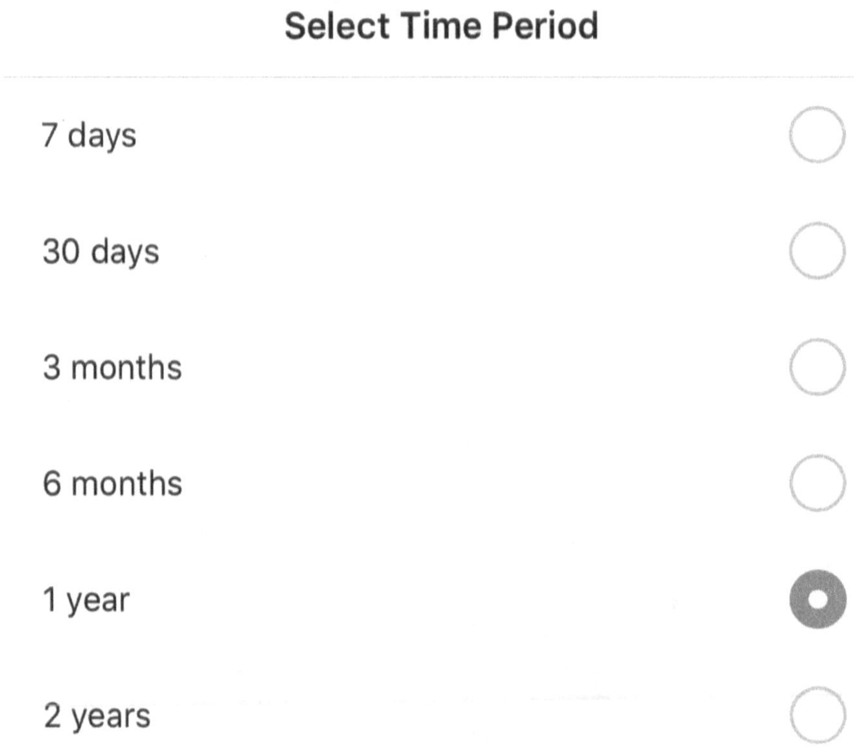

Select Time Period

7 days	○
30 days	○
3 months	○
6 months	○
1 year	●
2 years	○

And you can see the Interactions:

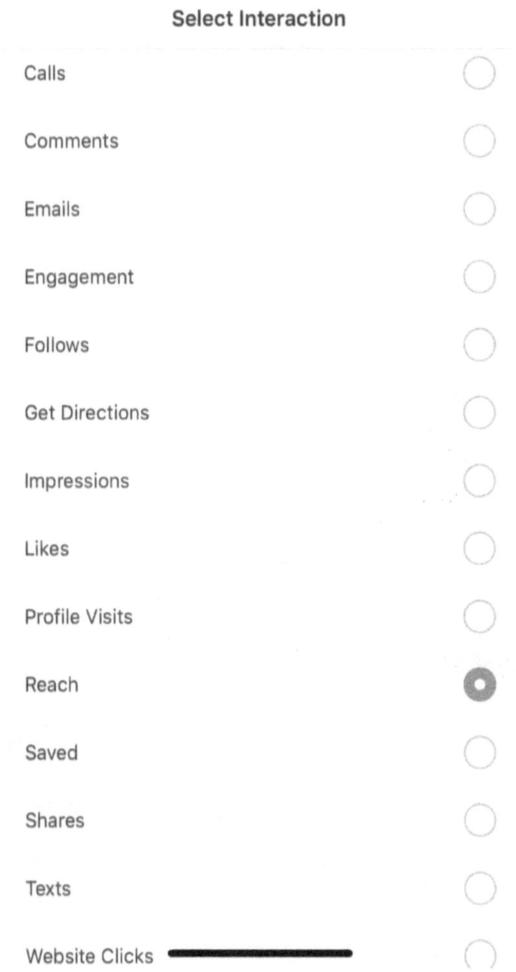

Select Interaction

Calls ○

Comments ○

Emails ○

Engagement ○

Follows ○

Get Directions ○

Impressions ○

Likes ○

Profile Visits ○

Reach ◉

Saved ○

Shares ○

Texts ○

Website Clicks ━━━━━━━ ○

Now you can slice and dice your posts, and have them sorted by Time Period + Type of Interaction.

This one is a period of 1-year and which posts made people want to go to my profile and click on my website to read the post:

I can see people enjoy sensational headlines "I was let go!" … "6-figure jobs that let you work from home!" .. and anything to do with making a lot of money and working very little - that seems to be my hook.

This one is over 1-year and which posts made people want to follow me the most.

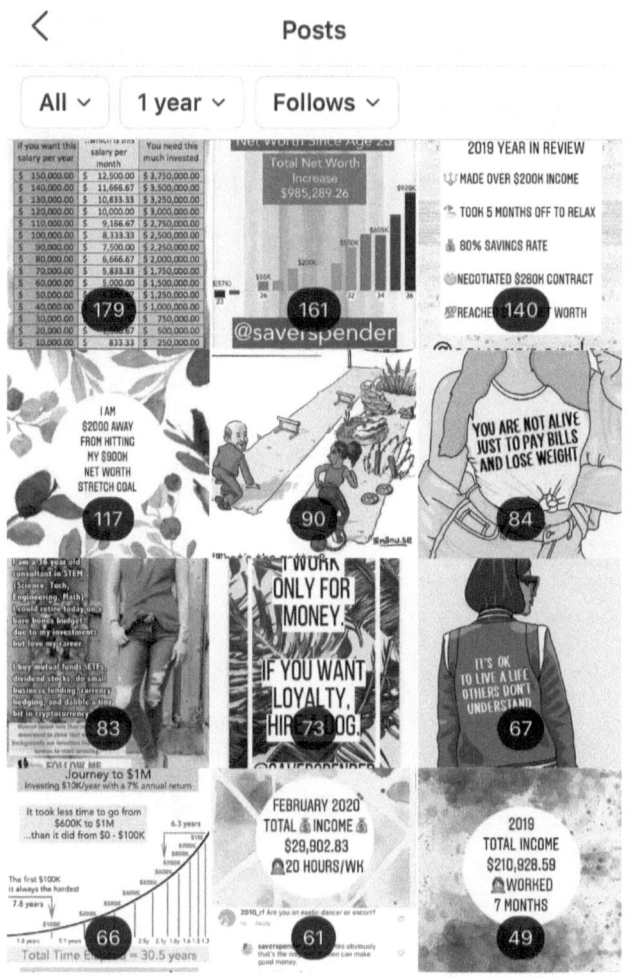

Some of these are evergreen posts that I can certainly redo and update to obtain more followers such as the charts, or an update on how my year went.

Under the **Activity** tab you can see what day you did best (Saturday for me in this case), and how much I have grown from week to week.

When I see these stats, I go to Saturday and analyze what I posted on that day that made me so popular, and I see what I can do to angle it in another way or to make a different variation on the post that would still seem fresh but obtain more followers.

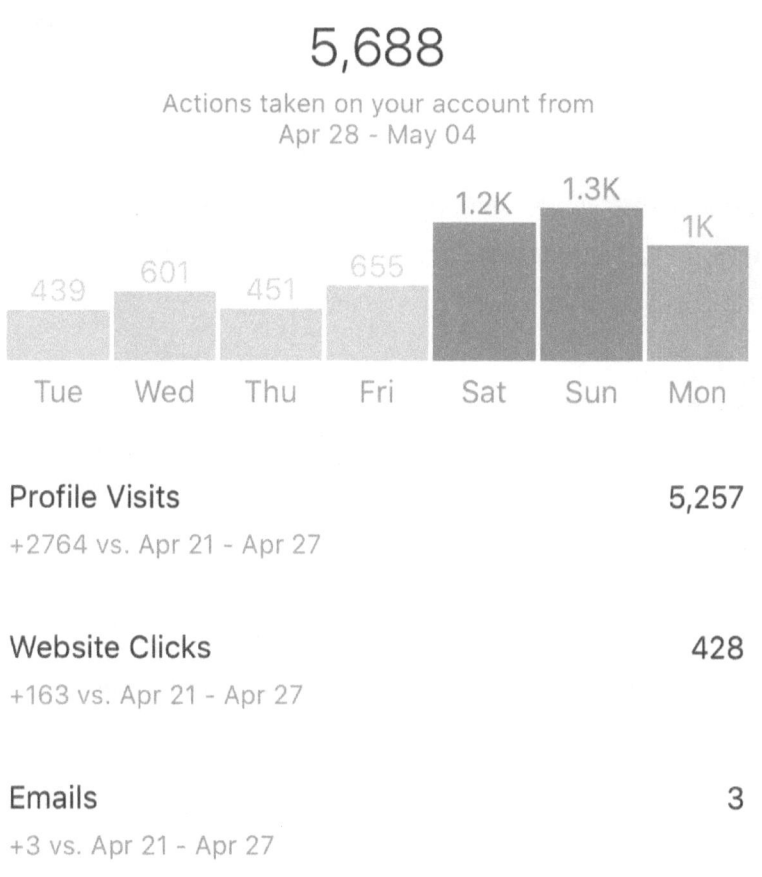

Interactions ⓘ

5,688

Actions taken on your account from
Apr 28 - May 04

439	601	451	655	1.2K	1.3K	1K
Tue	Wed	Thu	Fri	Sat	Sun	Mon

Profile Visits 5,257

+2764 vs. Apr 21 - Apr 27

Website Clicks 428

+163 vs. Apr 21 - Apr 27

Emails 3

+3 vs. Apr 21 - Apr 27

You can also see how your engagement pulled in people - obviously those same Saturday posts brought in residual interactions on Sunday and Monday, and the more I can capitalize on that to keep the momentum going with solid content, the better.

Pick an IG account to chase

This has always worked for me in school - to pick someone who was smarter at me in something and to work to try and beat that person in grades or whatever else.

It may seem silly, but putting an actual account/face/person to your goal, can help motivate you to do better and you can even spend time seeing what they do so well that you enjoy about their account, and try to replicate it in your own style for yourself.

I pick a few accounts:

Ones that are very close to me in followers, and I monitor how they are doing on occasion, and if I see they're doing well, it spurs me on to 'beat' their numbers.

I also aim higher, for ones that have 1000 - 2000 more followers than I have, and I don't check on them as often, but when I see a surge in my numbers, I go to their accounts to see how I am doing against them until I surpass their followers.

Try and stay consistent and motivated strictly by challenging YOURSELF to do better - it is not wrong to use tricks like benchmarking your account against others to see how you can do better and be more creative.

THE END

All of this has been a whirlwind of self-teaching, experimenting and trying out new ideas to see what worked and what didn't.

Not every IG account will be the same - yours will not be like mine, and mine is not like yours.

The key is to find out who your target market is and stick to them, stay true to your branding, and your core message, and most of all - be persistent and consistent.

A lot of promising IG accounts drop out because people can't sustain the momentum over a long period of time; think of it more as a marathon not a sprint, and don't get discouraged when things don't seem to be moving - all of your little actions are adding up to a bigger one.

I hope this book has helped shortcut a lot of what happens behind the scenes and how IG works, and the tips and tricks with all the apps (as free as possible) to make it work.

Drop me a line any time:

Sherry@SaveSpendSplurge.com

I'd love to hear from you!

(Really.)

ABOUT THE AUTHOR

Sherry is a 30-something professional entrepreneur who lives in Canada with her partner and toddler (whom she has affectionately nicknamed *Little Bun* on the blog).

She has been blogging for more than 10 years having started with clearing $60,000 of student debt in 18 months using *The Budgeting Tool* (TheBudgetingTool.com) which she now donates the net proceeds of to charity) to quadrupling her yearly income within two years of graduation and investing using *The Investing Tool* (TheInvestingTool.com).

This is the fourth book she has authored in the LikeaBossBooks.com series, and she has plans for many more.

She is work-optional meaning she doesn't need her job's paycheque any more, but loves it enough to keep going. Her side incomes bring in almost $50K a year now.

Sherry loves those rare, uninterrupted nights of deep REM sleep, stuffing her face with delicious food, and pretending she isn't secretly addicted to blogging and shopping for winter coats.

You can read more about this wealth-focused, style-obsessed, minimalist at her latest blog *Save. Spend. Splurge.* (**SaveSpendSplurge.com**).

Comments, and photos of adorable otters cuddling can be sent to:

Sherry@LikeABossBooks.com

@saverspender

Thank you!